X3

10/02

X3

10/02

Sunset

building
barbecues
&outdoor kitchens

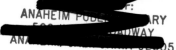
SUNSET BOOKS • MENLO PARK, CALIFORNIA

Sunset Books

Vice President and General Manager: Richard A. Smeby

Vice President and Editorial Director: Bob Doyle

Production Director: Lory Day

Art Director: Vasken Guiragossian

Senior Editor: Marianne Lipanovich

Building Barbecues & Outdoor Kitchens was produced
in conjunction with HomeTips

Editor: Don Vandervort

Coordinating Editor: Louise Damberg

Contributing Editors: Roy Barnhart, Steve Cory, Carol Crotta,
Derrick Riches, Charles Self, Peter Whiteley

Graphic Designers: Dan Nadeau, John Miller, Robin Ireland

Photo Director/Stylist: JoAnn Masaoka Van Atta

Illustration: Bill Oetinger

Book Designer: Robin Weiss

Production Coordinator: Patricia S. Williams

Assistant Editor: Bridget Biscotti Bradley

Proofreader: Lisa Black

Indexer: Rick Hurd

Cover: Design by Vasken Guiragossian. Photography by Ken Gutmaker.
Photo direction by JoAnn Masaoka Van Atta.

Cooking Outdoors

Backyard barbecues have come a long way since early charcoal braziers and hibachis became popular in the 1950s. Today, those once-simple grills have evolved into high-tech appliances designed to expand the kitchen out into the patio and garden. New outdoor cooking centers, which often include cabinets, refrigerators, sinks, and other amenities, serve practically and handsomely as focal points for entertaining.

The driving force behind the escalating popularity of barbecuing is its intrinsic appeal—the aromas, flavors, easy clean-up, and relaxed dining style that combine to create the "barbecue experience." There's nothing quite like a gathering of friends and family for alder-smoked Alaskan salmon or a sizzling London broil. Barbecuing, now more than ever, has become a great American pastime.

Although you can buy portable barbecues and ready-to-assemble outdoor kitchen islands from home improvement centers and barbecue specialty outlets, a more lasting—and often affordable—option is to build your own. That's where this book comes in. On the following pages, you will find ideas, plans, and complete instructions for building everything from simple firepits to complete outdoor kitchens.

THE FIRST STEPS

Before you embark on a barbecue-building project, you'll want to ask yourself a few questions so you gain a clear idea of the best approach for you. For example, do you want a simple patio grill, or a fully functional kitchen? How much space do you have available for a backyard cooking center? Is the area sheltered and close to existing plumbing, electrical, and gas lines? Do you want your barbecue to be built-in or movable? What sorts of appliances and storage do you desire? What are your year-round weather conditions?

Later in this chapter, we'll help you answer these questions, clarify your options, and plan a project that will fit your lifestyle, landscaping, home, and yard. Beginning on page 28,

you will find 16 building projects, complete with plans and detailed how-to instructions. A chapter on barbecue-building basics follows on page 94 to serve as a helpful reference for all types of barbecue projects. With your plan in hand, you can follow the directions to build a custom outdoor cooking area that will enhance the quality of your entertaining as well as the value of your home.

Considering the Possibilities

Depending upon your project's scope, an outdoor cooking center may require nearly as much consideration as a kitchen remodel. As with any project, the first step is to identify your needs. In other words, consider the kind of cooking you want to do, and on what

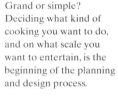

Grand or simple? Deciding what kind of cooking you want to do, and on what scale you want to entertain, is the beginning of the planning and design process.

scale you will do it. You'll also want to consider the climate and your family's lifestyle. Having a clear mental picture of these factors will help you narrow down the possibilities. Let's take a closer look:

COOKING STYLES AND CAPACITY: When most people use the term "barbecue," they actually mean grilling. Grilling is simply the process of cooking food over a high heat on a cooking grate. Barbecue, a style of cuisine that originated in the southern United States more than a century ago, is the process of slow cooking large pieces of meat in a smoke-filled chamber that burns hardwoods.

Today, any kind of cooking you can do in your indoor kitchen can be accomplished outdoors, often to greater effect. Wood-fired ovens allow you to bake breads, cook roasts, and even make pizzas; in addition to enhancing the flavor of the food, these ovens are more efficient than traditional electric ovens, providing better heat and air circulation for more even cooking.

The features and reliability of grills also have evolved, making them much more than just a place to cook steaks. Gas-powered burners allow you to fry, boil, and sauté a variety of side dishes, eliminating the need for trips to the kitchen.

Once you have determined the type or types of cooking you want to do outdoors, you need to consider the maximum number of people you will be cooking for on any given occasion. To help guide your design, plan out several sample meals. Make sure that your cooking center can handle the quantity of food and the required preparation, and that your entertaining area can comfortably accommodate your guests.

CLIMATE AND ENVIRONMENT: If you plan to cook outdoors year-round, your choices of appliances and materials will be influenced by your climate and location. You may need to winterize your cooking center, including insulating pipes and other lines. If you live by the ocean, you should consider stainless steel or other materials that resist the corrosive effects of salty air. If you have frequent winds, you may need to plan windbreaks to shelter your cooking area as discussed in the sidebar on page 24.

If you intend to locate your cooking center somewhere other than where you currently grill, make sure you are aware of the location's conditions at the times of day and times of year you plan to use it. Microclimates—the variation in climatic

Though little more than a counter and grill, this outdoor cooking center proves that an area need not be expansive to do the job.

conditions within your own property—can vary dramatically from one corner of a yard to another. Grilling in blistering heat or strong winds can quickly put a damper on the barbecue experience.

LIFESTYLE: Your outdoor cooking center should also reflect your household's lifestyle. How many members will be using the cooking center, how often, and what are their styles of cooking? Making sure your design accommodates a range of needs may make the difference between a unit that is used once a week versus one that is used once a month.

Unless you intend to enjoy the return on your investment entirely through the use of your new cooking center, it's a good idea to consider the market value of your home. If you build a very expensive unit in a relatively inexpensive neighborhood, you may not recoup your costs should you sell your home.

Be realistic about your willingness to maintain what you build. Depending on your climate and the size and use of your center, it may require frequent and thorough cleaning. In reality, how much time is your household prepared to devote to maintenance? For many people, the appeal of barbecuing is the ease of clean-up; if your center has almost all the features of an indoor kitchen, remember that it will require similar upkeep.

You also may want to consider alternative ways to use the cooking center, since these can have an impact on your design. For example, a wood-fired grill can double as a fireplace or fire pit. If family and friends enjoy sitting around a fire on cool evenings, consider a project that will accommodate this.

Reality Check

Once you have defined your cooking needs, your project will begin to take shape in earnest. But before you advance toward developing a design, determine how much of the project you can—or want to—do yourself and the resources you're willing to devote to it.

TIME: You will eliminate labor costs by doing the building yourself, but remember to place a value on your time. If, in a few hours, a professional can build a project that will take you several days, you might want to reconsider doing the work yourself unless you enjoy the process.

Also consider how much free time you have versus the amount of time you expect to spend on the project. If you only have a few

Stainless-steel cabinets and a tile countertop create a barbecue center that is both beautiful and easy to maintain.

hours a week to do the work, the building process may stretch out over several months.

MONEY: Develop a budget and stick to it. As with indoor kitchens, appliances easily can cost more than materials and labor. Knowing these costs upfront can help determine your choice of building materials so you can maintain your budget.

Even if you plan to do all or most of the work yourself, materials and appliances may not be your only expenses. You may incur costs for a designer, permits, deliveries, and tools. And you may find that you need to hire a professional for some aspects of the job, such as wiring or plumbing.

SKILLS: Later in this book, you will find detailed instructions on how to do the work yourself. You will see that, although none of the tasks is particularly challenging, some

require a little practice. If you lack experience in certain phases of a project, decide before you begin whether you want to learn the skills or hire a professional. In many cases, mistakes can be more costly than contracting out the work from the start.

In addition to being realistic about your skills, be realistic about any physical limitations you might have. Laying that first brick might seem easy, but by the time you get to the 200th one, it can feel like it weighs a ton. Pace yourself and plan plenty of time to rest between demanding aspects of the job.

TOOLS: Many phases of building your outdoor cooking center will require only very basic tools; however, you might need some specialized ones, too. Almost any tool you can think of is available for rent. See more about the tools needed for typical projects on page 96.

Property values are enhanced by an outdoor cooking center that integrates seamlessly into the landscape, as evidenced by this stucco-and-stone beauty.

CHOICES, CHOICES

As you move further into the planning phase of your outdoor cooking center, you'll need to make a number of choices—from the type and style of cooking unit to the materials and accessories that will define its look and functionality.

A variety of extras may expand a simple barbecue into a complete outdoor kitchen by providing for complete meal preparation and cleanup. These features may include a generous counter surface and sink, storage cabinets, and any of several useful appliances such as a refrigerator and side burners.

Just like your indoor kitchen, an outdoor cooking center should be designed to adequately house your equipment and to provide enough counter and work space for you to cook efficiently. Most structures are

ANATOMY OF A BARBECUE

A barbecue's construction depends largely upon whether it is classic or contemporary in style. A traditional solid-masonry wood- or charcoal-burning barbecue has a grill to hold the food and, below that, a shelf or grate to hold the fuel. Masonry firebox walls support the grill and the grate and contain the heat of the fire. If the grate is slotted, an open space below is usually constructed to serve as an ash pit.

But today's barbecues are seldom built in these traditional ways. With advances in technology, solid masonry barbecues have gone the way of masonry fireplaces. Prefabricated metal barbecues that fit within a masonry surround are now far more common. Most of these units have natural-gas or propane burners.

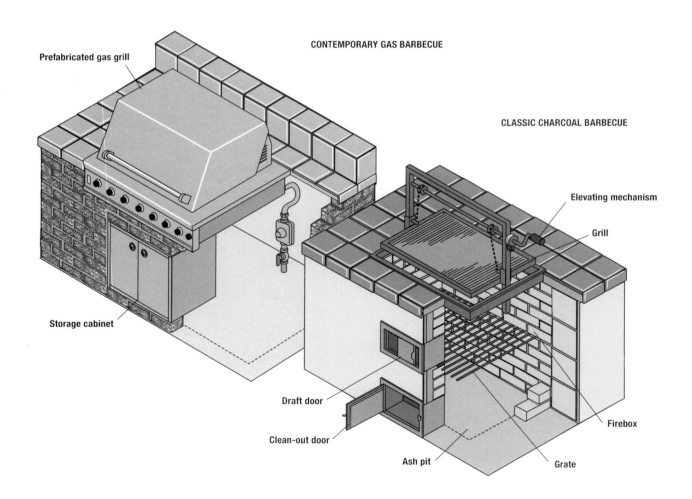

CONTEMPORARY GAS BARBECUE

Prefabricated gas grill

CLASSIC CHARCOAL BARBECUE

Elevating mechanism

Grill

Storage cabinet

Draft door

Clean-out door

Ash pit

Grate

Firebox

built to standardized specifications, not unlike the cabinets and counters in your kitchen. This way, they are not only comfortable to use, they will also accommodate standard-size appliances. For example, countertops should be from 32 to 36 inches high for comfortable use and at least 24 inches deep to adequately house grills and appliances. Depending on the scope of your project, your center may also require plumbing, gas, and electrical lines.

The materials for building a contemporary outdoor cooking center must be able to weather the elements as well as be suitable for the appliances you've chosen. For example, gas-grill inserts generate a great deal of heat, so they need to be framed using a non-flammable material.

The structural frame needs to be strong enough to support all the elements of the unit and to withstand the range of temperatures it will experience. Surface materials should be impervious to weather conditions, easy to maintain, and chosen to retain their appearance over time. While flammable materials can be used in the construction of a cooking center, they should not be used in any area that is exposed to high heat or flame.

Structural Materials

To choose materials for your barbecue, start by thinking about how the various choices will fit in with the style of your home. Incorporating similar colors and textures into your structure will enhance your property and its appearance. Look at the materials used in the construction of your house, garage, patio, deck, fencing, and any other structures on your property to get ideas for what you should use.

Once you've narrowed down your choices, visit your local home improvement center to begin pricing materials. Even if you haven't finally decided on the size of your cooking center, you should be able to compare the ultimate cost of different materials by their square-footage prices. You'll also want to be certain that whatever materials you choose are plentiful and readily available.

In addition to aesthetics, budget, and labor considerations, the size of your structure will influence the materials that are appropriate. For example, a large unit may require a concrete pad with brick or block support walls, while a smaller structure may only need a small footing with a block frame and wood supports.

BRICK: The durability, heat resistance, and aesthetic appeal of brick makes it an overwhelmingly popular choice for building barbecues. It provides a solid frame in which to install prefabricated appliances and on which to mount a countertop.

Brick's uniformity and ability to blend with a number of home styles makes it a favorite barbecue building choice.

CONCRETE BLOCK: Similar to brick in its structural properties, concrete block is an inexpensive and less labor-intensive alternative. It comes in an array of shapes and colors, as well as modular sizes. When fortified with reinforcing steel, concrete block can form one of the strongest and most durable of barbecue structures.

STONE: A little trickier than brick or block to work with because the pieces are not standardized sizes, cut stone provides an attractive alternative. The only disadvantage to working with stone is that it is porous and therefore must be treated to prevent staining from grease, water, and other substances. An alternative is to use synthetic stone tiles, which are more regular in shape and may be pretreated to resist staining

STUCCO: Usually applied over concrete block or brick, stucco gives a barbecue a finished look, especially when the home is also clad with stucco. However, because it requires the application of three coats—all of which require a period to dry, or cure—using stucco makes a project a relatively time-consuming process.

WOOD: A wood-frame structure is perhaps the easiest to build and allows for greater versatility in design, which can make the installation of appliances and utilities simpler. However, because wood is flammable, most grill-insert manufacturers specify that installation must not be in direct contact with wood. In addition, only wood that is naturally decay-resistant or has been pressure-treated will withstand the elements.

Concrete block offers ease of construction and high durability, but needn't look utilitarian. As shown below, split-face concrete masonry units can give an outdoor cooking center rugged, hand-hewn beauty.

Stone's natural appearance makes it perfect for rustic settings, though care in maintenance is a must.

When materials blend with a home's architectural style, an outdoor cooking center becomes an extension of the house. The wood barbecue, left, is smartly sheltered by an overhang; the stucco barbecue, above, resists harsh weather.

Surface Materials

The countertop of your outdoor cooking center needs to be resistant to your style of cooking as well as to the elements. If you plan on using the counter surface to prepare foods, you need to choose a material that will resist stains, germs, breakage, and the elements.

Solid-surface and laminate countertop materials are not recommended for outdoor use because they may deteriorate when exposed to intense sunlight, freezing temperatures, and heavy rain. Because wood is flammable, tends to expand and contract, and is difficult to keep clean its use it as an outdoor countertop choice is discouraged.

Stainless steel, while smooth, durable, and resistant to the elements, scratches easily and can heat up mightily in warm weather, making it impractical.

Stone and tile are the overwhelming favorites for countertops:

GRANITE: Granite is far and away the best stone choice for a countertop; however, it is also the priciest. It is naturally resistant to heat and stains, is smooth, easy to clean, and very durable. For more about granite and related materials, see page 101.

SLATE: A less expensive alternative to granite, slate is a less even surface and must be treated before it is used. Depending on the size of your countertop, you may be able to find a single piece at a stone yard or quarry that is large enough to provide full coverage.

ARTIFICIAL STONE: Though most is manufactured for indoor use, artificial stone, with the proper treatment, may be acceptable for an outdoor countertop. Be sure to ask the supplier or manufacturer before purchasing.

GLAZED TILE: Tile resists heat and the elements and offers an array of design options, making it easily the most popular choice for outdoor areas. A nearly endless array of patterns, colors, textures, and finishes is available. For more about tile, see page 103.

UNGLAZED TILE: Its rustic look makes unglazed tile a popular choice for patio pavers, but it is very porous and must therefore be treated with a sealer to prevent staining and the spread of germs when used as a countertop material.

Glazed tile, available in a vast selection of color, texture, size, and price, is the most popular choice for outdoor countertops.

Slate, directly below, provides a rustic look but tends to produce a somewhat uneven surface; it should be sealed to resist stains. Granite, shown at bottom, is the densest, most water-resistant, and costliest of stone tiles.

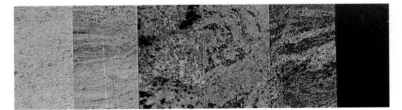

Appliance Choices

The growing popularity of outdoor cooking has inspired a whole new generation of appliances. Once you have determined the types of cooking you want to do in your outdoor center, you're ready to shop. Let's take a look at the currently available products and custom options, from a simple charcoal grill to everything you'd need for a full outdoor kitchen.

Grills come in charcoal, gas, and electric varieties, and in a range of shapes and sizes. All operate efficiently and effectively, so choosing one basically boils down to personal taste.

While charcoal provides the best "out of doors" flavor, gas is cleaner and faster to work with; electric grills are simple to operate and maintain but provide even less flavor. In recent years, the manufacture of smoker trays designed to hold fragrant wood chips has greatly added to the popularity of gas grills.

CHARCOAL GRILLS: Anyone who has ever visited a campground has probably seen the most basic grill there is. A charcoal grill is simply a receptacle for coals or wood chunks with a cooking grate suspended above. Of course, there are improved versions of the traditional charcoal barbecue, and they produce sophisticated results. The array of options includes adjustable fireboxes, rotisserie mountings, multi-level cooking grates, vented lids, and more. Most of these are designed to provide the cook with greater heat control.

Charcoal imparts excellent flavor that can vary depending upon the type of charcoal (or wood chunks) you burn. Charcoal grills are also easier to build because they don't require hookups for gas or electricity (unless power is needed for rotisseries or other features). On the downside, you have to deal with bags of charcoal, starters, and less control over the heat.

You can construct a "garage" around a

Charcoal grills, whether freestanding, below left, or built-in, above, embue foods with outstanding barbecue flavor. In addition, charcoal eliminates the need for gas tanks or lines. Choose a charcoal unit that offers convenient ash removal and fire control.

freestanding grill, or you can install a grill unit into a structure you build. If you opt for the former, remember to plan for adequate airflow through the fire and cooking area. If you decide to install an insert, obtain the exact design specifications from the manufacturer before you finalize your plans, and have the grill on hand before you begin construction. A proper fit is critical to the appearance, performance, safety, and maintenance of your grill.

A quality charcoal grill is constructed of powder-coated or porcelain-enameled steel. The grate may be porcelainized or nickel-plated, to resist rust and clean up easily, or bare cast iron, which sears meat wonderfully but must be oiled regularly to prevent rusting. In either case, the more closely spaced the bars of the grate, the better. Finally, make sure to check out the grill's ash-removal system, which may affect your construction plans.

With their ease of use, efficiency, and cleanliness, gas grills are a favorite choice. High quality gas-grill inserts, such as the one shown below, can be costly but are worth the investment because replacement of a lesser model can be difficult. Constructing a "garage" for a freestanding unit, such as the one shown above right, gives you all the benefits of a built-in, along with portability.

GAS GRILLS: The convenience and cleanliness of gas make it the most popular grill choice. With the growing popularity of custom outdoor cooking centers, most gas grill manufacturers have introduced a line of grill inserts. These drop-in or slide-in units tend to be pricey, but for good reason. They are usually made from high-quality stainless steel and carry long-term warranties. When comparison shopping, pay particular attention to the warranties, especially for mechanical failure. Removal and replacement of a grill insert can be difficult, so the more reliable and reparable the unit the better in the long run.

If you have ever used a freestanding or cart-mounted gas grill, you know its drawbacks—lack of work space and the nuisance of having to periodically unhook and fill up the propane tank. Gas-grill inserts allow you to control the shape, size, and materials of the surrounding work area, and most of them can be hooked up to your home's gas line. In addition, side burners can be attached to the insert, eliminating the need for extra trips to the kitchen.

A large number of insert units are

currently available, ranging from small and simple to large, full-function units. A quality model is made from coated steel, which holds up better than painted aluminum, with porcelain-coated cast-iron or stainless-steel burners that generate 25,000 or more BTUs. Heat is generated through a distributor or by ceramic briquettes, charcoal-looking briquettes, or lava rocks.

Gas units are fueled either by natural gas or liquid propane (LP), sparked by an electronic igniter. Of the two, natural gas is more convenient—you don't need to buy and/or refill fuel tanks—but more difficult to install because it requires a gas pipe that connects to your home's gas supply. Piping natural gas to the unit isn't always feasible and, in the case of portable units, makes it impossible to relocate the barbecue.

Removable bottoms and specially designed grates that catch and vaporize drippings are two features worth looking for since they substantially ease cleaning chores.

ELECTRIC GRILLS: Though electric grills are available, they can be difficult to find because they represent less than 3 percent of the barbecue market. Electric grills are as simple in design and use as an electric oven. A switch-controlled heating element provides the "flame" and cooks the food in much the same way as your oven's broiler. Most require a dedicated electrical circuit and must be UL approved for outdoor use.

A quality electric grill should have a porcelain steel body and porcelain grate. Most important, the lid should be lined with an aluminum composite to allow the heat to reach temperatures hot enough for searing. This lining also helps to distribute the heat

Electric grills provide for clean, no-fuss barbecuing—you just plug them in.

evenly while insulating the unit as well.

The primary advantage of electric grills is the ease of cleanup and the convenience of the power source.

SMOKERS: These are the appliance of choice for people who like to go whole hog—literally. If you are interested only in smoking cuts such as briskets or rib backs, it's best to invest in a freestanding commercial unit. They come in varying sizes, in electric or gas models, and a sign of quality is

The kamado cooker combines the best of a charcoal grill and a smoker, allowing the chef to efficiently slow-cook smaller cuts of meat.

a powder-coated steel body and chrome grates. If, on the other hand, you want to roast an entire pig some day, you will definitely need a large smoking chamber.

Building a smoker is a straightforward project, requiring a firebox in which you can build a smoky fire, a smoking chamber for the food, and a stack to provide ventilation and draw the smoke from the firebox over the meat and out. Typically, smokers are built from brick or stone, which absorb and radiate heat much better than does metal. A smoker can be either vertical or horizontal, depending on your space.

FIRE PITS AND FIREPLACES: Fire pits and fireplaces are built for aesthetics as much as for function. A fire pit is basically a hole in the ground with a decorative stone or brick ring constructed around it; an outdoor fireplace is much the same as an indoor one, just with less need of venting.

These simple structures are often used as a focal point for a relaxing post-dinner evening under the stars, but they can also be used for serious cooking. Harkening back to the earliest cooking fires, they can be equipped with spits, tripods, cooking grates, and rotisseries. If you decide to construct

Smokers are generally for the barbecuer who likes to eat and entertain in a big way. Be sure to check with your local fire department about any restrictions governing their construction or use.

one, at the very least make sure you invest in some long metal skewers for roasting marshmallows and cooking hot dogs.

A number of prefabricated units also are available. They come in steel or a variety of masonry materials and have porcelain-treated grilling surfaces. With many models, the grill can be removed after cooking, and a screened enclosure and lid transforms the unit into a fireplace.

OVENS: Whether fired by wood, charcoal, or gas, outdoor ovens can cook anything your kitchen oven can, but with the advantage of radiant heat. From Indian tandoors to Italian pizza ovens, there are many types you can build, but the basic principle remains the same—fire-heated ceramic material radiates heat evenly and intensely throughout the food.

The standard design of a live-fire oven is a stone box with an access door in front. The fire is built in the center of the oven, and after the interior becomes hot, the fuel source is pushed to the side. The food is placed where the fuel source used to be, and the food is then cooked by the heat radiating from the stone.

Other styles of ovens, like the tandoors of India, have openings at the top, and the food is lowered inside on long metal skewers. Or, like Chinese ovens, the food is placed on grates above the fire. You can also build a warming oven adjacent to your grill or smoker to keep foods warm while you cook other dishes.

Several manufacturers offer oven "kits" that come with all the parts for the oven itself, including the clay crown elements, flue manifold, terra-cotta brick, and iron door. The kit includes directions for the unit's foundation and surround but does not include the materials for these.

A fire pit (at left), though commonly used as an outdoor fireplace, can be equipped to cook anything you would on a grill.

Outdoor ovens can deliciously bake everything from pizzas to meats—slowly and evenly with radiant heat.

Outdoor Kitchens

Today, just about any amenity you can have in your kitchen is available in an outdoor version. Stainless-steel cabinets withstand the elements and are sufficiently weather tight to store food and supplies. Sinks, refrigerators, and side burners are now being made strictly for outdoor use.

When choosing a location for your outdoor kitchen, keep in mind that it will require full utility hookups for sinks, grills, and electrical appliances. Because it will be subject to weather conditions, be particularly careful to site it for minimum exposure. You may also have to erect windbreaks or other structures to provide for protection.

Be certain that any appliance you plan on installing outdoors be manufactured for that purpose. A reliable way to tell is to look for the UL (Underwriters Laboratory) seal approving it for outdoor use. Standard indoor appliances are not rated for the kinds of conditions outdoor equipment will experience, and they can be hazardous if installed outdoors.

Fortunately, the growing popularity of outdoor cooking has spawned a whole new generation of appliances (many of which were originally designed for use on boats). They include:

Though this outdoor kitchen appears beautiful enough to have indoors, all construction and appliances were carefully chosen for outdoor use.

ROTISSERIES: These units, especially when directly wired to a power source, allow you to cook a wide variety of foods effortlessly. Units that mount directly into a hooded grill make cooking even more convenient. A ½-inch-thick stainless-steel rod resists rust and can easily handle 40 pounds of food.

VENTILATION HOODS: You might not think it necessary to install a ventilation hood over your grill, but this is an essential element if you are placing a grill beneath a patio roof or similar shelter, and particularly if the grill does not have a cover-type hood. A ventilation hood helps vent smoke away from the cooking area, can provide a light source for cookouts after dark, and protects against fire. Hoods for outdoor use are generally made from stainless steel, but porcelain-coated steel and steel with tile finishes are also available.

SIDE BURNERS: A wide variety of electrical and gas side burners are available, in single or double units. They can be attached directly to the grill unit or inset in a counter. Side burners allow for the complete preparation of a meal outdoors, allowing the cook to greatly expand the types of foods that can be prepared.

Quality models have heavy-duty porcelainized removable grates with stainless steel supports and bowls for easy cleaning. The units are made of stainless steel, have solid-brass valves and output 15,000 BTUs or more of heat.

When choosing a rotisserie, make certain the rod can support the weight of the foods you plan on cooking and that the unit is easily removable for cleaning.

Ventilation hoods, far left, increase safety from flare-ups and prevent smoke from pervading the dining area. Side burners, left, offer a secondary surface for cooking or warming foods. They should be designed for easy cleaning, with all removable parts, and come with stainless-steel covers.

Because of its beauty and resistance to the elements, stainless steel is far and away the favorite for outdoor cabinetry, above, sinks and faucets, far right, and refrigerators, bottom right.

that is not plastic will work. A gooseneck or arching spout with a single handle is very popular for outdoor use.

REFRIGERATORS: A wide variety of manufacturers make refrigerators for outdoor use. Most are constructed of stainless steel and have tempered glass shelves. The great majority are front-vented, under-counter units, which can be built into the grill center, where they receive added protection from the elements.

CABINETS: Typically made of stainless steel, outdoor cabinets also come in wood or enameled porcelain finishes designed to withstand direct exposure to the elements. Outdoor cabinets are similar to indoor units in size and construction, and can be mounted above or below a countertop. They generally are not specially insulated, but contents can be protected with latches that create a tight seal.

SINKS AND FAUCETS: An outdoor sink allows for easy and immediate cleanup and is a source for water needed in the preparation of various foods. Most outdoor sinks are made of stainless steel, but almost any sink that will not be damaged by temperature changes, such as enameled cast iron or composite, will do the job. When choosing the size of sink, think about how it will be used and select accordingly. Any type of faucet

DESIGN CONSIDERATIONS

Once you have decided on the elements of your outdoor cooking center, page through this book to see if you can find a project that is similar. Keep in mind that you can modify these projects, adjusting the materials and techniques as needed. If you can't find a project that suits you, put together a design of your own or have a professional draw up a set of plans.

Be sure to consider how and where the center will fit into your property, any legal and safety issues, and the availability of utilities such as electricity, gas, and water.

Location

When planning your outdoor cooking center, consider the style and location of your house and other structures on your property, your yard's natural traffic patterns, the location of utility hookups, and prevailing weather conditions.

Open flames need to be far from flammable overhangs, trees, fencing, and decks. An already-existing patio is a natural choice because of its proximity to the house and utility hookups, but you will need to examine the space with a critical eye, locating your grill away from your house's eaves and cutting back tree branches to a safe height.

While guarding against the risk of an open flame will be the primary safety consideration in your planning, it's not the only one. How will traffic flow around the cooking area? Will people be forced to pass close by to get to the house or yard? Do children play nearby? Be sure to consider safety first when choosing a location.

Once you have chosen your location, rope off the area to get a feel for the space the center will consume. Take note of how

you move around this area now. Will it inhibit your traffic patterns? Will it obstruct a view?

Visit the area several times throughout the afternoon and evening. Does it receive consistent wind or none at all? What is the exposure to the sun? Remember that the sun's angle and arc change with the seasons—it has a high arc in summer and a lower arc in winter. Avoid a western-facing cooking center so you won't be blinded when cooking with the sun low in the sky.

Codes and Regulations

While there is no national standard regulating grill construction, local ordinances in some areas restrict the conditions or locations that you can have an outdoor fire. Factor these into your safety considerations during your planning.

REGULATIONS: Save yourself time and frustration by checking with your local planning department before finalizing your plans, and certainly before beginning construction. Your local authorities can also provide you with minimum safety standards. If you are planning to build a fire pit or fireplace, contact your local fire marshal's office to obtain information on what you can burn and when you can burn it.

Also investigate your area's zoning laws, which might restrict the size, use, and placement of your structure. Most areas restrict how close to property lines you can build. Though you probably won't encounter any restrictions at all, it's good insurance to check first.

Depending on the scope of your project, you may also need to obtain building permits.

Many areas require permits—and may require plans—for electrical and plumbing work. If you are planning to install a manufactured insert, you may need to supply the unit's specifications. Because permit fees usually are calculated as a percentage of the total estimated construction cost, accurate figures are important.

SAFETY: Every unit needs to be properly vented so heat can dissipate quickly and thoroughly after use. Also, be aware of the potential for hot spots in your cooking units—for example, a smoker's firebox will cause one side of the unit to become extremely hot.

Gas-burning units should be installed strictly according to the manufacturer's specifications, which are developed to prevent gas from accumulating inside the unit. In addition, only use the type of fuel recommended for the unit. If you use propane (LP) gas tanks, be sure to store them in a place where the temperature does not exceed 125 degrees Fahrenheit and away from sharp or jagged edges that can puncture the tank or damage the lines.

Planning for Easy Care

Even the most basic outdoor cooking center requires cleaning, and even the best grill inserts require maintenance. To make your care and maintenance chores simpler, consider which materials will be the easiest to clean of smoke and soot. Fireboxes should have an easy clean-out access port for the removal of ash.

If you live in a climate with freezing temperatures, plan to winterize your grill. It doesn't take much for water pipes to break in freezing conditions, so if your center has a faucet or other water sources, design in drains that allow you to clear all water from the system. Water connections should be buried below the frost line, as should gas lines. If you are unsure about how to do this work, consult with your local building department and consider hiring a professional to set up the basic utilities.

The structure you build will need protection from the elements as well. Exposed wood will need to be sheltered from a hot

SCREENING AGAINST WIND

Too much wind can create enough chill on cool days to make an outdoor dining area unusable. A solid vertical barrier may not be the best choice for modifying the effects of mild prevailing breezes; angled baffles, lattice-type fencing, or deciduous plantings will disperse wind better. To determine whether areas need to be sheltered from the wind, post small flags or ribbons at various places on your proposed site and take note of their movements during windy periods.

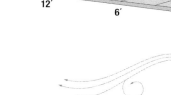

Solid vertical barrier
Protection drops off at a distance roughly equal to the barrier's height.

12′   6′   0′

Solid barrier, baffle angled into the wind
Good protection near the barrier, to a distance twice the barrier's height.

12′   6′   0′

Spaced-wood screen or lattice
Wind diffused near the screen, best protection 6 to12 feet from the barrier.

12′   6′   0′

Solid screen, baffle angled toward the barbecue area
Best protection up to 8 feet from a 6-foot-high barrier.

12′   6′   0′

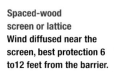
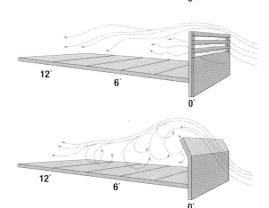

sun to prevent drying and cracking. And it must be protected from moisture—usually with hardy paints or stains—to prevent rot. Metal parts must withstand corrosion from humid or salty climates. Stainless steel is a good choice for such areas because of its durability in these conditions. Other metals should be galvanized, primed, and painted for protection.

Lastly, make sure all cracks and separations between materials are sealed properly with a silicon sealant to prevent water from getting in between the parts. Even small amounts of moisture can cause corrosion or cracking, particularly if the water freezes, compromising the integrity of the structure.

Utility Connections

Any utilities you connect to your cooking center must be installed with the utmost regard for safety. Electrical wiring should be routed to your cooking center via approved electrical conduits to ensure that the wire itself is protected from the elements or breakage. Electrical receptacles must be the ground-fault-circuit-interrupter (GFCI) type to allow the power to be shut off imme-

diately in the advent of a short. And, they should be protected by waterproof electrical box covers. If you have any doubts about doing this type of work yourself, hire a licensed electrician to accomplish it or to look over your work and the system before you power it on. (For more on installing electrical wiring, see page 136.)

Gas lines should be inspected from end to end to make sure that all fittings are tight and there are no leaks. To do this, turn on the gas and brush the length of the line with soapy water. If bubbles appear, you have a leak. Never use a match or flame to test for leaks. Most gas companies will send someone out to inspect your work to make sure that it's safe.

Though a water leak is not immediately dangerous, be as careful installing plumbing lines as you would installing electrical or gas lines. Slow-dripping water inside your structure can quickly erode mortar and rust metal parts in places you cannot see, eventually compromising the entire structure and its safe use. For more on installing plumbing and gas lines, see pages 131–135.

Natural gas, piped to your barbecue's location, offers a permanent, low-maintenance solution to fueling the flames. The gas pipe's outlet should have an exterior shutoff valve.

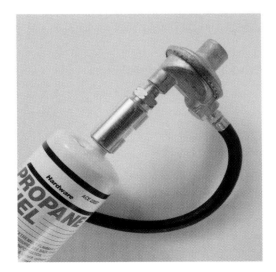

Where natural gas isn't available—or would be difficult to run to the barbecue—consider opting for a liquid propane (LP) system, as shown in the photo at left.

MAPPING A DESIGN

As you look through the projects in this book, it is unlikely that any one of them will fit your backyard and needs exactly. Adapting a design to your specifications is a simple matter if you break it down into stages.

The Basic Design

The best way to start designing your outdoor cooking center is to draw a complete map of your yard on graph paper, as much to scale as possible. (Use the largest sheets you can find since the larger the scale, the easier it will be to visualize the structure.) Be sure to include overhanging structures and trees so you can pinpoint the best location.

Next, map out an area larger than what you will need to give yourself plenty of room to adjust the positions of the various components. Then make several sketches of your center, positioning its elements in different configurations.

A scale drawing is the first step toward developing a workable plan.

If you find it hard to visualize from drawings, mark off the area in your yard with some wooden stakes and string once you have the basic shape drawn. Examine the traffic flow, any obstruction of views, and sun and wind exposure. Make any needed adjustments, reductions, or expansions.

The Final Plan

Once you've chosen your materials and appliances, you can put together your final plan. Precision is crucial at this point. The plans must include the exact dimensions of the materials you use. For example, keep in mind that a 2 by 4 is usually not 2 inches by 4 inches, but rather $1\frac{1}{2}$ by $3\frac{1}{2}$ inches (see page 94 for more about materials). Check with suppliers to make sure the materials you are planning on using are the measurements you have specified.

Unless your cooking center is very simple, it's a good idea to employ an architect or draftsperson to help draw or at least check your plans. This is particularly important if you will be contracting out any of the work—though you will know what you were thinking when looking at your own plans, a contractor may not. This can lead to mistakes that literally can become set in stone.

Working with Professionals

No matter how skilled a builder you are, there are occasions you may need to hire a professional. Finding the right help is as important as any other part of the process, but before you even start your search, carefully and completely define this person's role, determine at what stage in the project you will require these services, and figure out how much you can afford to pay.

It's also wise to find the professional or professionals you need before you start the project because they often can give you information and advice on preparation and construction techniques that will make their work easier and, therefore, less costly. Always get at least two detailed and complete bids for a job and ask to see examples of previous work.

Finally, ask for references and call them. If you are having premade components installed, speak with local distributors. You can also contact local trade associations or building departments for recommendations, and most local builders can usually put you in touch with satisfied customers.

With any professional you hire, make sure all the terms of the contract are put in writing, provide as much direct supervision as you can, and never pay more than 10 percent of the total fee in advance. Following are the various professionals you may need:

ARCHITECTS AND LANDSCAPE ARCHITECTS: Unless your project is very complex, you probably won't need an architect to plan your design. Most landscape architects can help you put your plans together and site your project. Both are state-licensed, have professional degrees, and are trained to create designs that are structurally sound, functional, and aesthetically pleasing. They also are knowledgeable about construction materials, can negotiate bids with contractors, and supervise the actual work.

DRAFTSPERSONS: A draftsperson can draw up a formal set of plans, which might be required if you need any building permits and which will likely be requested by any contractor. For adapting any of the plans in this book, a qualified draftsperson is probably your best choice.

CONTRACTORS: Like architects, general contractors are state-licensed, bonded, and carry their own workmen's compensation insurance. If you decide to use one, find someone who specializes in outdoor construction. If you only plan on hiring someone to do a specific job, such as masonry, plumbing, or electrical, make sure you find someone who specializes in that area. Plumbing and electrical contractors should be licensed; masonry contractors are not required to be. Contractors and other building professionals generally can order materials at better prices. Always request a sample of the material, and make sure that what is ordered is the quantity and quality you are expecting.

SOIL ENGINEERS: If you're planning on building a large or unusually heavy masonry structure on unstable soil or a steep lot, you may require the services of an engineer. These specialized professionals, many of whom can be found through local government offices, can evaluate your soil conditions and establish design specifications for foundations or footings.

HANDYPERSONS: Handypersons are often a good and inexpensive choice for building a small barbecue or similar project because they may be adept at a variety of tasks. On the other hand, unless they come highly recommended, you don't know what you're getting. No license or particular training is needed, so buyer beware.

Barbecue Projects

One sure way to ease the job of building a new barbecue or outdoor kitchen is to start with a good plan. In this chapter, you will discover 16 plans for building all types of barbecues and outdoor kitchens, from a simple "garage" for a portable grill to comprehensive centers with every amenity—including the kitchen sink. You'll even find a bonus plan for a classic barbecue that ran in one of *Sunset*'s earliest books.

Each project includes photographs of the finished unit and text that points out design details and step-by-step construction techniques. "Exploded" or cut-away illustrations give you an overview of each project's construction; elevation, section, plan, and detail drawings offer dimensions and additional useful information.

You'll also find a "Materials Checklist" with each project that specifies the primary materials you'll need to buy when you visit your home improvement center and/or barbecue specialty retailer. We expect that you will want to adapt a plan to suit your yard, budget, needs, and tastes, so quantities and sizes of materials are not listed in most cases. No matter what project you tackle, be sure it will meet all local building codes.

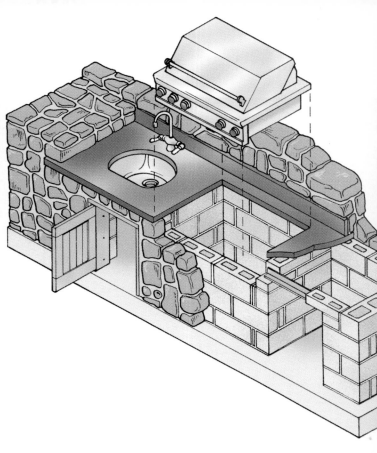

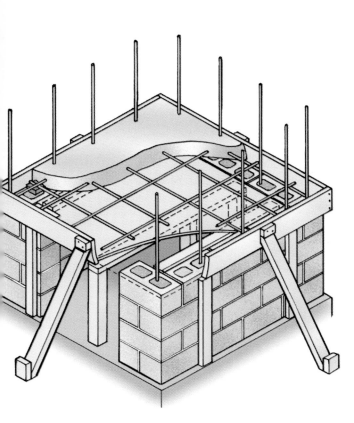

SMALL SLATE BARBECUE

A compact slate barbecue turns a garden corner
into a classy outdoor cooking center.
Landscape architect: David Fox

A stainless-steel gas grill with rotisserie is the key feature of this compact garden barbecue. Slate tile covers the walls and counter, and a custom copper door, crafted by a metal artisan, accents the barbecue's façade. The barbecue is designed as a companion to the fire pit project on page 66.

Design Details

Beneath this barbecue's slate exterior is a concrete-block structure perched on a reinforced concrete foundation. The slate counter is applied with a bed of mortar to heavy-gauge stainless-steel sheeting, a substrate that is not only strong and durable but non-combustible.

A gas pipe fuels the barbecue grill and an electrical outlet serves up power to the rotisserie. The metals used on this unit—stainless steel for the grill and copper for the door—are impervious to rust. The grill's gas valve can be easily accessed through the copper door in the ample storage area beneath the barbecue.

Building Notes

Before starting construction, buy the grill and have it on-site so you can double-check the size of the recess as you build. The door should be made by a metal shop after the structure has been built so the fabricator can fit it precisely. At the same time, have the fabricator measure and cut heavy-gauge stainless steel for the countertop base. Note that stainless steel can be pricey so you may want to opt for one of the other countertop constructions discussed on page 124. If you decide to use another material, be sure to check if you will have to modify the plans.

Cut the slate tile with a masonry blade mounted on a power circular saw or rent a "wet" tile-cutting saw with a diamond blade. Be sure to wear safety glasses when cutting.

1 Excavate an area to form a reinforced concrete foundation as shown in the illustration on page 32. The barbecue featured here has a 12-by-12-inch perimeter footing and a 6-inch-thick concrete slab. Strengthen the footing or slab by running $1/2$-inch steel reinforcing bars horizontally through the footing and in a grid pattern every 12 inches in the slab. Cut the reinforcing bar with a metal-cutting blade mounted on a circular saw (be sure to wear gloves and safety glasses) and support the grid about 3 inches off the ground with fragments of bricks or broken concrete blocks. Also run reinforcing bars vertically at the corners, as shown in the illustration on page 32.

2 Have a plumber rough-in a gas line for the grill, located as specified in the owner's manual that comes with the grill. Place a gas shutoff valve where it's easily accessible through the metal door. Also have an electrician stub-up conduit and wiring for an electrical receptacle. The conduit should be located where it can run through the concrete block cells to the receptacle. Locate the receptacle where you'll be able to easily plug in the rotisserie if your grill has one.

3 When the utilities have been roughed-in and the steel is placed, cast the concrete foundation and slab as discussed in the directions on page 110.

MATERIALS CHECKLIST

Gas grill

Prehung custom copper door

Gas pipe, shutoff valve, & connections

Electrical conduit, cable, boxes, & GFCI receptacles

Ready-mix concrete (or concrete ingredients)

Lumber & plywood or scrap for concrete forms

$1/8"$ hardboard for concrete forms

$1/2"$ & $3/8"$ steel reinforcing bar

Concrete blocks

Mortar mix for concrete block

$3" x 3"$ angle iron

Heavy-gauge stainless-steel sheeting

Thin-set mortar (for surface tile)

Slate tile

Tile spacers

Stain-resistant grout for tile

Grout sealer

Tile & stone sealer

Various masonry screws & concrete nails

4 Build the concrete block walls as discussed on page 120. As you build, place $1/2$-inch steel reinforcing bar vertically in every other cell and lay a $3/8$-inch reinforcing bar horizontally along every other course. Check each course with a level as you work. Leave openings for the door and a recess for the grill. Use angle iron to support half-high blocks that bridge the doorway (see page 118). Use the portable circular saw equipped with a metal-cutting blade to cut the angle iron.

5 Scrape excess mortar from the joints as you work. After you've laid all the blocks, fill the cells with grout (see page 104), making sure not to grout the cells where electrical conduit runs.

6 Allow the grout to set up. Then build the base for the countertop slate. Mortar the sheets of heavy-gauge stainless steel in place on the top course of concrete blocks (or use an alternate countertop construction, as discussed on page 31).

7 Cut in a rectangular hole for the receptacle's electrical box and mount the box on the conduit (see page 136). Using a hand grinder with a masonry-cutting blade to cut this hole is easiest.

8 Install the slate tile on the walls working from the bottom right corner of one side and moving upward and across the wall. Trowel mortar onto the blocks and the backs of the slate, then press each piece of slate into position. Seat each piece by gently tapping it with a rubber mallet. Don't apply mortar to more concrete blocks than you can cover in about 20 minutes. Keep joints between slate straight and uniform (you can use plastic tile spacers for this).

9 Lay the countertop slate using the same methods as those for the walls. Do a dry run before permanently setting the tiles to work out the most attractive arrangement of patterns and diminish the need for cutting.

10 After the mortar has dried completely, mix and apply grout (see page 128). Allow the grout to dry.

11 Set the grill into place and connect it as discussed on page 131. For information on installing a receptacle, see page 136.

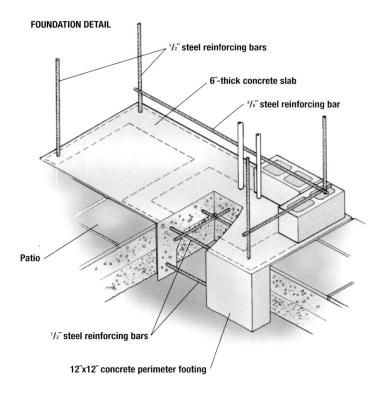

FOUNDATION DETAIL

$1/2$″ steel reinforcing bars

6″-thick concrete slab

$3/8$″ steel reinforcing bar

Patio

$1/2$″ steel reinforcing bars

12″x12″ concrete perimeter footing

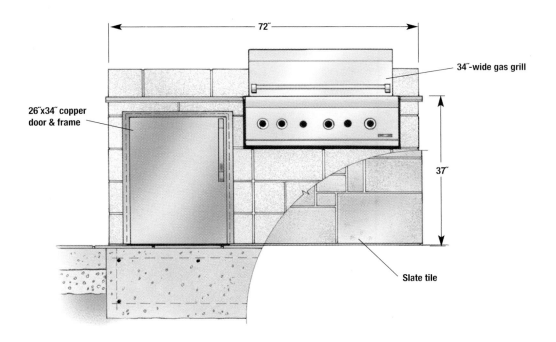

72″

34″-wide gas grill

26″x34″ copper
door & frame

37″

Slate tile

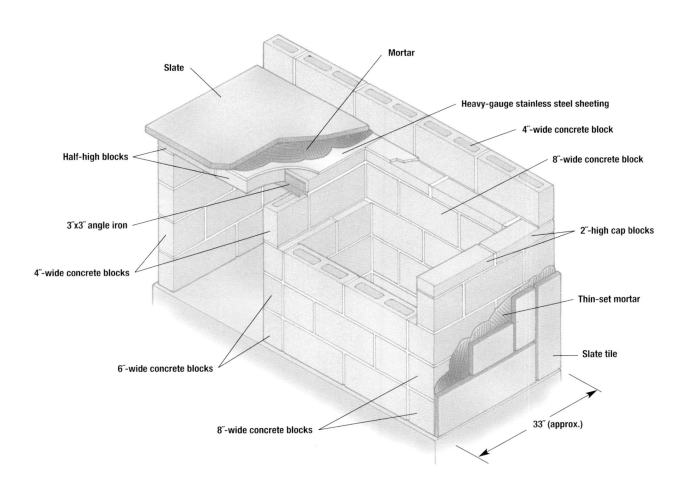

Slate

Mortar

Heavy-gauge stainless steel sheeting

4″-wide concrete block

8″-wide concrete block

Half-high blocks

3″x3″ angle iron

4″-wide concrete blocks

2″-high cap blocks

Thin-set mortar

Slate tile

6″-wide concrete blocks

8″-wide concrete blocks

33″ (approx.)

COBBLESTONE CHARCOAL BARBECUE

This 4-foot-by-8-foot cobblestone barbecue features a ceramic tile countertop that offers more than 10 square feet of space on each side of the recessed grill. Below the counter, weather-tight cabinets built into the diagonal walls provide ample storage.
Landscape architects: Lauderbaugh/Hill Associates

Perhaps the most interesting feature of this built-in charcoal barbecue is its recessed fire pit and custom-made adjustable-height grill. To fabricate a similar unit, you must locate a foundry (probably one that is experienced in making barbecues).

Design Details

To modify this design, you could easily equip the unit for gas instead of charcoal and build a cover for the fire pit when it is not in use.

The barbecue sits on a 4-inch-thick reinforced concrete slab, which in turn is supported on a footing that extends to the area frost line. See more about forming footings and foundations on pages 110–111. Extending the slab beyond the barbecue to form a patio is optional.

Building Notes

To make the counter height a comfortable 36 inches tall, you must choose stones that will result in walls about 33 inches tall, allowing 3 inches for the 2-by-8 cap and countertop (depending on the tile thickness). By choosing stone sizes carefully, varying course heights, and adjusting the size of mortar joints, you can limit the amount of stone and masonry cutting.

1 Before you lay the stone and masonry units, build the two cabinets and doorframes that are set into the diagonal corners. Use ³/₄-inch B-C or A-C exterior-grade plywood to construct the carcass (box). Cut a plywood shelf or two for each and install them on 1-by-2 cleats. Use pressure-treated 2 by 6s to construct four-sided doorframes. Hold the frame

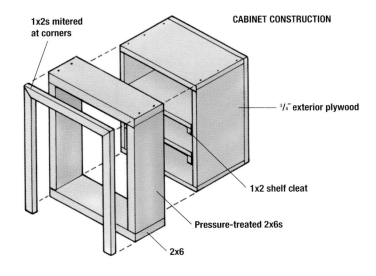

CABINET CONSTRUCTION

1x2s mitered at corners

³/₄˝ exterior plywood

1x2 shelf cleat

Pressure-treated 2x6s

2x6

square with a temporary diagonal brace or piece of plywood tacked to the edge. Size the opening to suit the stone course height. Anchor the doorframes with masonry screws, recessed from the face of the wall and flush at the back of the wall. (After the walls are constructed but before the counter is installed, attach each cabinet to its base and doorframe.)

2 Lay the first course of stones up to the doorframes. While not as regular as masonry units, cobblestones are fairly square and so require more mortar than brick but less than other more irregular stones. Leave a space for the cleanout door (a standard item at a masonry supply), centered on the front or back, as you wish. Mortar the door in place. Attach metal brick ties to the back of the door jambs with exterior screws and embed the other ends of the ties in the mortar joints as you construct the wall. (Alternatively, attach the frame with masonry screws into the cured mortar joints.)

3 Now build the internal walls of the ash pit, which also form the foundation for

MATERIALS CHECKLIST

Lumber & plywood or scrap for concrete forms
Crushed stone
Ready-mix concrete
6˝ reinforcing wire
Concrete blocks
Firebricks
Refractory mortar for firebrick
Cobblestones
Lime-free mortar mix for stone
Cast-iron cleanout door & frame
¹/₂˝ steel reinforcing bar
8˝ anchor bolts
Pressure-treated 2x6s & 2x8s
Marine-grade plywood (³/₄˝)
Waterproof membrane
Brick ties
Various screws & nails
Thin-set mortar (for surface tile)
Glazed exterior tile
Stain-resistant grout
Grout sealer
18˝x24˝ doors & hardware
1x2 redwood
Custom-made grill

the fire-pit hearth and walls. For a 3-foot-wide finished fire pit width lay two courses of concrete block spaced 44⅝ inches apart (outside dimensions) and extending between the front and rear stone walls. Grout the cells solid as you complete each course.

4   Lay the next course or two of stone until the top is level with the top of the block walls. Set seven 32-inch-long #4 steel reinforcing bars (½-inch diameter) on 4-inch centers between the two block walls and resting at least 3 inches on the front and rear stone walls. These bars support the double-course firebrick hearth as it extends over the ash pit. At the same time lay another full course of stone.

5   Lay a course of firebrick to cover the entire area from the outside edges of the block walls, and between the stone walls build a firebrick wall, leaving a brick out as needed to provide an ash-dump slot. Spread a setting bed of mortar over the bricks, and lay another layer of brick perpendicular to the first layer. Complete the fire pit by laying a single-wythe brick wall around the perimeter. Adjust mortar joints as needed to extend to the planned height. Now complete the stonework. As you lay the top course, embed anchor bolts in the mortar joints to secure a pressure-treated 2-by-8 cap. Level the top of the wall with a bed of mortar.

6   Allow the masonry to cure overnight before you install the cabinets. Screw through the cabinet floor into the treated 2-by-6 base and through the plywood

sides into the doorframes. Trim around the door openings with 1-by-2 redwood, mitered at the corners. Install the cabinet doors with galvanized butt hinges and add galvanized pulls.

7   Install a pressure-treated 2-by-8 cap on the top of the wall flush with the outside edge. For each anchor bolt, counterbore a 1½-inch hole to recess the washer and nut, and bore a ½-inch hole all the way through. Then cut off the bolts flush with the top of the nuts using a hacksaw.

8   Use minimum ¾-inch marine-grade plywood as a base for the tile counter. It should extend to the outer edges of the 2-by-8 cap and to within about an inch of the fire pit opening on all sides. Spread a thin layer of latex-modified thin-set mortar over the plywood and cover it with a waterproof membrane. Then set tile (suitable for exterior use) in the same thin-set, as discussed on page 127. Extend edge tile ¾ inch past the edge of the plywood base, and fill under the overhang and against the edge of the plywood with mortar. Grout with an epoxy or other stain-resistant grout, then apply the recommended sealer.

9   Measure the inside dimensions of the fire pit for the three-piece custom grill. The specifications given on the facing page may be helpful. The fire grate is #4 steel bar welded on 1-inch centers to a #4 bar frame and supported on steel legs. When sizing the grate, leave enough clearance so it can be tilted on edge when you need to sweep ashes into the ash dump.

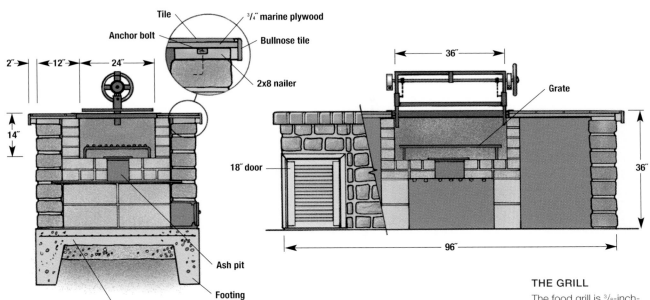

Tile

Anchor bolt

¾″ marine plywood

Bullnose tile

2x8 nailer

2″   12″   24″

14″

36″

Grate

18″ door

36″

96″

Ash pit

Footing

4″ concrete slab

THE GRILL

The food grill is ³⁄₈-inch-diameter steel bar welded on 1-inch centers to 1-inch-square tubular steel frame. The upper assembly lifts out as a unit. It consists of 1½-by-1½-inch steel angle, which edges the perimeter of the fire pit opening. The grill frame is welded to the angle at the center of each side. The frame supports a ½-inch-diameter steel wheel shaft with a turning wheel on one end and a winding drum with a steel link chain on the other.

Tile

Thin-set mortar

Waterproof membrane

Thin-set mortar

¾″ marine-grade plywood

Pressure-treated 2x8 cap

Anchor bolt

½″ steel reinforcing bars

Cleanout door

Ash pit

Firebrick

Firebrick

Cobblestones

Concrete blocks

BARBECUE ISLAND FOR A PORTABLE GRILL

This "barbecue garage" is not only easy to construct,
inexpensive, and lightweight, it has the added benefit of
keeping your grill portable.
Designer and builder: Peter O. Whiteley

Here's a way to enjoy the advantages of a built-in barbecue at a fraction of the cost of most outdoor cooking centers—a multifunctional, freestanding "parking structure" for the ubiquitous portable gas grill. Covered in gauged green slate tiles, the garage has the look of a built-in. In addition to masking the barbecue's frame, wheels, and propane tank, the shell provides a buffet counter and a storage cabinet for cooking supplies. Be sure to have your gas grill on hand before planning and building the unit.

Design Details

For safety, the gas-grill industry recommends a 24-inch clearance between a propane-fueled grill and any combustible material, such as wood. For that reason, this unit has non-combustible framing made from steel studs covered with fire-resistant cement backerboard.

The steel-frame construction makes this barbecue particularly lightweight. In fact, the basic framework is light enough to be built in a shop or garage and carried to the final location. For that reason, the unit doesn't need a substantial foundation—just a flat slab, such as a patio, will do.

Building Notes

Steel studs are surprisingly easy to work with. Available at building supply centers, they're competitive in price with wood but are much lighter. Use a circular saw with a composition metal-cutting blade to cut them to size. The vertical studs slip into horizontal U-shaped channels used for the top and bottom of the frame. Self-drilling screws designed for steel framing, instead of nails, hold the pieces together.

The backerboard, sold in the tile section at home centers, is available in 3-by-5-foot panels and in $1/4$- and $1/2$-inch thicknesses. The lighter weight $1/4$-inch panels are used on the sides, and the top is covered with a $1/2$-inch panel. The backerboard can be scored and snapped, or cut with a saw blade designed for cutting concrete and stone.

In addition to a few standard carpentry tools (see page 97), you'll want to have a bucket or wheelbarrow (for mixing mortar and grout), rubber gloves, a rubber-backed trowel, a bag of plastic tile spacers, and a notched trowel with $1/4$-inch teeth. It's a good idea to rent a tile saw for cutting the slate.

Building the Shell

As shown on page 41, four rectangular stud walls screw together to form a P shape. To stiffen the frame and support the backerboard for the top and floor, it is spanned with cross-braces formed by steel studs.

1   Measure the length and width of your grill, plus the height of its work surface. For adequate clearance, the "parking space" should be 2 inches longer and wider than the grill itself. For the front side, add 24 inches for the storage end. The finished counter height should be level with the barbecue's work surface, so account for the thickness of tile and the top piece of backerboard when determining the frame height.

2   Cut the studs and channels for the front, back, and sides. The door for the storage compartment goes on the front. Its opening has a horizontal header flanked by pairs of studs, their solid sides facing out.

MATERIALS CHECKLIST

Six 10'-long, $3/8$"-wide steel studs

Three 10'-long steel channels

$3/4$" self-drilling metal screws

Four 3-by-5' sheets of $1/4$" backerboard

One 3-by-5' sheet of $1/2$" backerboard

Backerboard screws

4' of 1x12 rough-sawn redwood (door)

Paint or gray semitransparent stain (optional)

4' galvanized metal or zinc strap hinges

Wood screws

Galvanized metal door pull

Cabinet door catch

Thin-set mortar (for surface slate)

1'-square slate tiles

Tile spacers

Sanded grout

Tile & stone sealer

Each pair measures 3⅝ inches from the outside edges—the width of a stud. Add a third stud next to the inner pair to create blocking to which you will screw the back panel of backerboard.

3   Butt and screw both sides to the front so the outside edges are flush with the outer edges of the pairs of studs flanking the door opening, then attach the back.

4   To provide surfaces for attaching the floor, cut pieces of scrap channel to fit between all the studs that frame the bottom of the storage area. Offset them upside down over the bottom channels; attach with screws through the sides.

5   For cross-braces, cut four 20-inch-long pieces of stud material. Cut 1½-inch slits along the creases on both sides of each end to create two tabs. Space these crosspieces equally, fold their tabs out, and screw them in place.

6   Cut ¼-inch backerboard to cover the sides; secure it to the frame with backerboard screws. Cover the top and floor with ½-inch backerboard (notch the bottom to fit around the studs). Screw it in place with backerboard screws.

7   Cut two pieces of redwood to length and width so that, side by side, they make the door for the storage cabinet. Join these with wood cleats across the back. Attach hinges to the studs with metal screws and to the face of the door with wood screws. Add a handle and catch. Install the door after the barbecue's exterior is finished.

Covering the Frame

If you live in an area subject to freezing temperatures, be aware that backerboard manufacturers cannot guarantee that tiles will remain adhered. Consider covering the sides of your barbecue garage with stucco, cement-based siding panels, or artificial stone, or create a board-and-batten look with backerboard. For other countertop options, see page 103.

Many tiles are appropriate for outdoor use (see page 14). Slate tile was selected for this project because the visible edges look attractive, eliminating the need for any edging or corner tiles. See page 127 for information about applying tile.

To minimize tile cutting, place whole tiles at each corner of the top of the storage cabinet, overhanging the sides by the thickness of the tiles so they serve as a cap for the side tiles. Calculate the size of the tiles that must be cut to fit between the whole ones, allowing for grout lines. Plan the placement of the tiles on the remainder of the top. Also plan to continue the grout lines from the top surface down the front (some trimming of tiles may be required); an attractive option is to offset the middle band of tiles, as has been done in this project. Plan the layout of the remaining vertical surfaces, leaving a ⅛-inch gap at the bottoms.

When you're sure your plan is correct, cut all partial tiles (see page 128), double-checking the fit as you go. Mix mortar, then set the tile in mortar in stages, starting with the countertop. Use plastic tile spacers to create even grout lines and to hold the bottom band of tiles off the ground. When the mortar is dry, mix and add grout. When the grout is dry, seal it with a grout sealer.

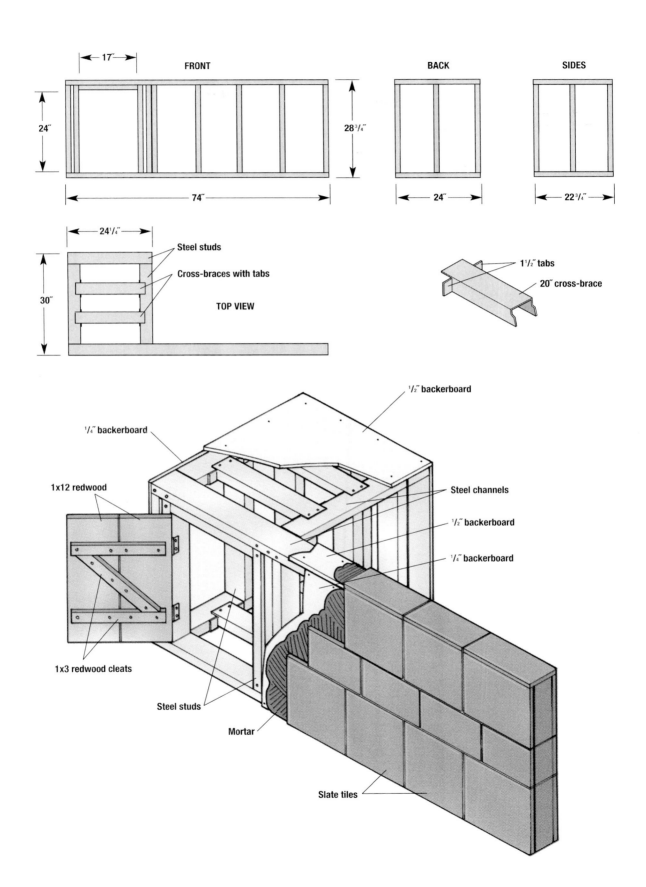

← 17″ →

FRONT

BACK

SIDES

24″

28³/₄″

74″

24″

22³/₄″

24¹/₄″

Steel studs

Cross-braces with tabs

30″

TOP VIEW

1¹/₂″ tabs

20″ cross-brace

¹/₂″ backerboard

¹/₄″ backerboard

1x12 redwood

Steel channels

¹/₂″ backerboard

¹/₄″ backerboard

1x3 redwood cleats

Steel studs

Mortar

Slate tiles

RELAXED ELEGANCE

Large and thick limestone tiles on a stuccoed structure
make for a solid, handsome, and functional outdoor
cooking and dining center.
Landscape architects: Peter Koenig Designs
Mason: Steve Marquoit

In this combination cooking/dining center, one counter is used for dining and the other for food preparation. A gas grill is positioned so that the cook stands facing guests—perfect for conversation and food service. The 44-inch-wide stainless-steel grill handles even large cookouts with ease.

Design Details

The design has a simple, uncomplicated look. Behind the stucco wall surfaces, concrete blocks provide sound construction. For the countertop, 2-inch-thick Arizona flagstone rests on a substrate (slab) of 3-inch-thick reinforced concrete. The flagstone counter cantilevers out 9 inches to provide leg room for diners. Below the flagstone, a row of $1/2$-inch-thick matching trim tiles covers the edge of the concrete substrate.

Building Notes

Purchase the grill and stainless-steel access door beforehand, and build the walls to fit. (The access door is for reaching the gas line's shutoff valve in case of emergency, not as an entryway to storage space.) Wait to order the flagstone for the counter until after you have cast the counter's concrete substrate. Then have the stone dealer cut the thick stones to size and fit.

For cutting the thinner stone trim tile, it's a good idea to rent a "wet" tile-cutting saw that pours water across the diamond blade as it cuts. To cut or trim the Arizona flagstone yourself, you can use either of two methods. One is to score a line by tapping a 3-inch stone chisel lightly across it, then follow along the line with harder hammer strokes on the chisel until the piece pops in half. Another is to score a $1/2$-inch-deep cut

across the stone using a hand grinder equipped with a masonry-cutting blade; center that cut so it teeter-totters over a length of 3-by-3-inch angle iron set on flat ground, then break both halves downward.

1 Pour a concrete slab (see page 110) to support the structure. A 6-inch-thick slab strengthened with a grid of $1/2$-inch steel reinforcing bar every 12 inches will satisfy most codes and provide a sturdy base. Use a power circular saw fitted with a metal-cutting blade to cut the steel. Run gas and electrical lines through the slab (see pages 131 and 136–137) and, using a sweep L fitting, run the electrical conduit straight up about 4 feet, where it will pass through the cells (holes) in the concrete blocks as they are stacked.

2 Build the concrete block walls (see page 120), reinforcing each course with $3/8$-inch reinforcing bar placed horizontally across the centers of the blocks. The portion that supports the dining countertop is five courses high; the portion supporting the cooking area is four courses high (see the illustration on page 45). Leave an opening for the barbecue unit, sized exactly according to the manufacturer's specifications. Frame an opening for the access door, and support the blocks across the top with angle iron as discussed on page 118. At the location of the electrical conduit, slide the concrete blocks over the conduit, then, at the top block, cut a hole and mount an electrical box (see more about this on page 136). It's easiest to use a hand grinder with a masonry blade for making the cutout.

MATERIALS CHECKLIST

Gas grill (with storage cabinet)

Prehung stainless-steel door

Gas pipe, shutoff valve, & connections

Electrical conduit, cable, boxes, & GFCI receptacles

Ready-mix concrete (or concrete ingredients)

$1/2$˝ & $3/8$˝ steel reinforcing bar

Concrete blocks

Mortar mix for concrete block

3˝x3˝ angle iron

Lumber & plywood or scrap for concrete forms

3˝ screws

$1/2$˝ concrete backerboard

Mortar (for flagstone)

2˝-thick Arizona flagstone

$1/2$˝-thick x 4˝ stone tiles

Stain-resistant grout

Sand stucco mix

Tile & stone sealer

3 Fill all the concrete block cells with concrete. Scrape the joints, but don't bother striking them since the block will be covered with stucco.

4 Cut pieces of $1/2$-inch concrete backerboard to form the base for the countertop slab. Trowel mortar on top of the blocks, and set the backerboard in the mortar. The backerboard should overhang the wall $1/2$ inch in most places, so it will be flush with the wall once $1/2$ inch of stucco is applied. At the side and end where diners will sit, the backerboard should cantilever about $8^1/2$ inches, to allow for leg room. On the lower countertop, cut an opening to accommodate the barbecue unit. Remember that the stone tiles will overhang the slab by $1^1/2$ inches on all sides.

5 Build 2-by-4 forms for the countertop's concrete slab. See the illustration at right and page 92 for instructions on supporting the framing. The poured concrete will be 3 inches thick—the width of a 2 by 4 minus the thickness of the backerboard.

6 Where the countertop cantilevers out to provide leg room in the dining area (see the bottom illustration on the facing page), make the forms by screwing together two pieces of 2 by 4—one flat and one on end. Support these pieces with vertical 2 by 4s. Check all the forms to make sure they are level and sturdy.

7 Lay a grid of $1/2$-inch reinforcing bar on top of the backerboard, crisscrossed every 12 inches. Pour the concrete, lifting the rebar up to the center of the slab as you pour. Strike and trowel the concrete until it is level and fairly smooth. Once the concrete sets, remove the forms. Allow the concrete to cure for several days before laying the tile.

8 Coat the outside of the concrete block walls with stucco, following the directions on page 119, and allow the stucco to dry thoroughly before proceeding.

9 Install the barbecue unit and the stainless-steel access door, following the manufacturer's directions.

10 Lay the flagstone tiles on top of the counter slab in a dry run to check for fit. Make any necessary cuts as discussed on page 43. The tile should overhang the countertop slab by 1 to 3 inches.

11 Remove the flagstone, keeping track of each piece's position. Mix and trowel on a $1/2$-inch-thick mortar bed (see page 127). Set the tiles in the mortar, maintaining even gaps between them.

12 Trowel mortar onto the edges of the counter's slab and set trim tiles in it. Support the tiles until the mortar has set by placing 2 by 4s horizontally beneath them and nailing 2-by-4 legs onto the temporary supports.

13 Wait a day or two for the mortar to cure, then apply grout to the countertop and trim tiles (see page 128). After a few more days, apply silicone sealer to the tiles according to package directions.

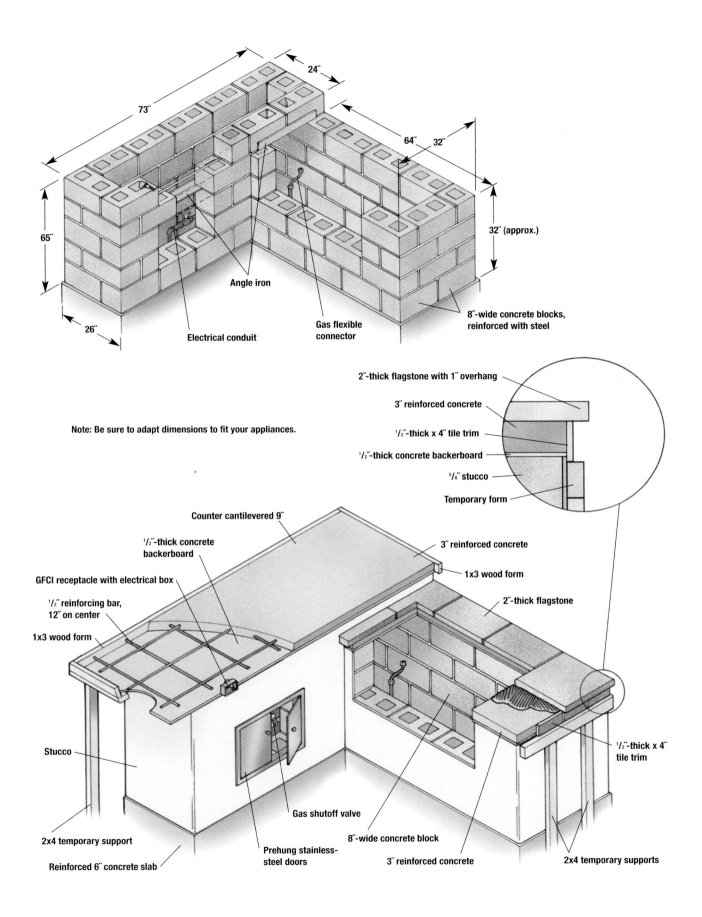

24"

73"

64" 32"

65"

32" (approx.)

Angle iron

Electrical conduit

Gas flexible connector

26"

8"-wide concrete blocks, reinforced with steel

Note: Be sure to adapt dimensions to fit your appliances.

2"-thick flagstone with 1" overhang

3" reinforced concrete

1/2"-thick x 4" tile trim

1/2"-thick concrete backerboard

5/8" stucco

Temporary form

Counter cantilevered 9"

1/2"-thick concrete backerboard

3" reinforced concrete

GFCI receptacle with electrical box

1x3 wood form

1/2" reinforcing bar, 12" on center

2"-thick flagstone

1x3 wood form

Stucco

1/2"-thick x 4" tile trim

2x4 temporary support

Gas shutoff valve

Reinforced 6" concrete slab

Prehung stainless-steel doors

8"-wide concrete block

3" reinforced concrete

2x4 temporary supports

OUTDOOR INDOOR KITCHEN

This barbecue center brings the good looks of indoor cabinetry to a site notched into a hillside. Because it's made primarily of wood, this type of unit is suggested only for mild-weather climates
Designer: Allison Rose

Built to look like a free-standing kitchen island, this tile-topped center sits on a deck with a post-and-beam foundation and has a built-in sink, gas-fired grill, side burners, and electrical outlets.

Design Details

The white-painted cabinets stand on thick legs so they appear less massive and more furniturelike. The 93-inch-long middle section houses the drop-in grill and side burners; the flanking 55-inch-long wings feature the sink and faucet plus generous food-preparation space. Doors with inset beaded paneling provide access to under-counter storage areas.

Building Notes

The 36-inch-tall center has a plywood top covered with concrete backerboard and tile, but in freezing climates, it's best to lay a level mortar bed into which the tile top and edge trim will be set.

This project is designed for do-it-yourselfers with intermediate woodworking skills and a good assortment of tools, including a table saw. You can cut and assemble parts of the barbecue center in a garage, but due to its finished weight, final assembly must be done on-site. Permits and inspection of plumbing and wiring by local building officials will likely be required.

Building the Frame

1 Rip three sheets of $^3/_4$-inch plywood into $23^1/_4$-inch panels. On one, lay out a full-size drawing of the center section, including the flanking pairs of 4-by-4 legs. The ends of the center section angle inward at $67^1/_2$ degrees and will cover half of the legs beneath it. On a second panel, lay out the bottom of the cabinet and notch around the legs. Also mark the outline of the opening needed for the drop-in barbecue unit.

2 Using two of the remaining ripped pieces, lay out the flanking sides, including the center pairs of legs. Note that the outer ends are square and the inner ends are at $67^1/_2$ degrees. Lay out the bottom pieces for each side on the remaining panels.

3 Cut eight $34^1/_4$-inch-long 4-by-4 legs. Using the full-size drawing of the top as a guide, cut two lengths of 2 by 4s to make the top and bottom pieces that span between the back pair of legs. (Their ends should be angled with a $67^1/_2$-degree cut.) Cut another 2 by 4 to make the bottom front crosspiece. Following the same drawing, cut the horizontal 4 by 4s that will support the drop-in grill.

4 Mark points $4^1/_2$ inches from the bottom of each of the legs. Attach the horizontal 2-by-4 bottoms with deck screws at an angle. Add the remaining 2 by 4 to the rear legs so it's flush with their tops.

5 The grill will rest on a $^3/_4$-inch plywood shelf spanning between the horizontal 4 by 4s. To locate these pieces, you must take into account the thickness of the tiles, the mortar bed, the plywood top and shelf, and the manufacturer's specifications for the depth of the unit. After making these calculations, attach the boards together with waterproof glue and deck screws at an angle.

MATERIALS CHECKLIST
Gas grill with side burners
Stainless-steel sink, faucet, & plumbing
Gas pipe, shutoff valve, & connections
Electrical conduit, cable, boxes, & GFCI receptacles
Exterior plywood ($^3/_8$" & $^3/_4$")
2x4 & 4x4 lumber
1x2, 1x4, 1x6, & 1x8 face-frame wood
Dowels
Beaded-board paneling
Waterproof glue
Various deck screws & nails
$^1/_2$-inch concrete backerboard
Thin-set mortar (for surface tile)
Countertop tile
Tile spacers
Stain-resistant grout for tile
Grout sealer
Rust-resistant hinges & door hardware
High-quality exterior finish

6 Complete the center frame by adding top and bottom horizontal 2 by 4s that will connect the front and back leg sections.

7 Cut out the top and bottom plywood pieces. From scrap ³/₄-inch plywood, cut the shelf for the grill as well as the side and back pieces that will fit vertically between the grill shelf and top.

8 Rip a 30¹/₂-inch-wide panel of ³/₈-inch plywood to cover the rear frame from leg to leg, check for square, and nail it in place.

9 Place the remaining pairs of 4-by-4 legs flat on a work surface, spaced according to the plan drawings of the end cabinets. Cut 2 by 4s for the top and bottom end rails and attach. Cut the front and back pairs of 2 by 4s that will span from the end legs to the center section and attach.

10 Cut the plywood tops and bottoms for the end sections and attach, then cut the back and end panels from ³/₈-inch plywood and mount them to the frame.

The Face Frame

1 Cut two 4-by-35-inch pieces from 1-by-6 framing wood. Center, glue, and nail them over the middle pair of front legs. Then cut two 5¹/₂-by-35-inch pieces for the outside end legs from 1 by 8s and tack them in place over the ends of the cabinet shells.

2 Make the horizontal face-frame members. To do this, measure the distance to the boards facing the inner legs and add 1 inch. Rip two pairs of boards to measure 5¹/₂ and 1³/₄ inches wide. Cut one end of each board at 67¹/₂ degrees so the angled ends butt snugly against the inner legs. Mark where the ends meet the outer legs and cut them square. Remove the end legs and these crosspieces. Join the horizontal boards to the vertical ends with countersunk dowels. Glue and nail to the front face of the side cabinets.

3 Cut a 5¹/₂-inch-wide bottom piece for the face frame to fit between the center pair of legs.

4 The size of the Y-shaped upper part of the face frame for this section will be dependent upon the size of the barbecue unit. Allow room for two pairs of 12-by-16-inch doors and a center spine, as well as the U-shaped panels that wrap around the bottom and sides of the barbecue.

The Doors

1 Rip 1-inch stock to measure 2 inches wide. Cut a ¹/₂-inch-deep, ³/₄-inch-wide rabbet along a back edge of the boards.

2 Attach the doors to the frames with dowels and glue the pieces together.

3 Cut panels of beaded board to fit in the frames. Glue and tack them in place.

Finishing the Unit

To protect the unit from weathering, apply a high-quality outdoor finish. Discuss options for the material you've used with your paint dealer. Tile the top as discussed on page 127 and install the grill, plumbing, and wiring (see pages 131–137).

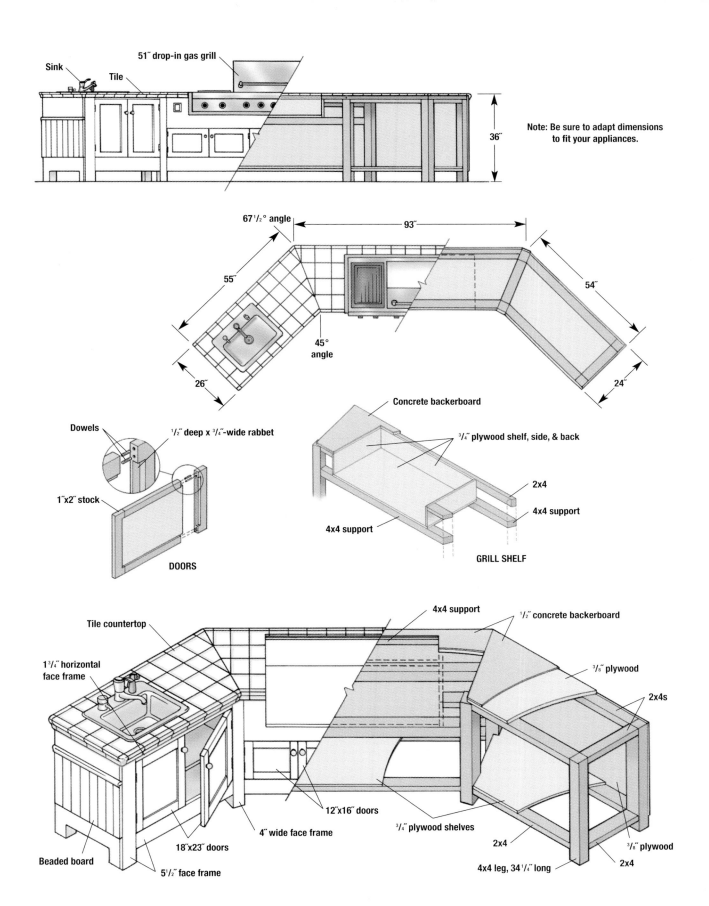

Sink

Tile

51″ drop-in gas grill

36″

Note: Be sure to adapt dimensions to fit your appliances.

67 1/2° angle

93″

55″

45° angle

54″

26″

24″

Dowels

1/2″ deep x 3/4″-wide rabbet

Concrete backerboard

3/4″ plywood shelf, side, & back

2x4

4x4 support

1″x2″ stock

4x4 support

DOORS

GRILL SHELF

Tile countertop

4x4 support

1/2″ concrete backerboard

1 3/4″ horizontal face frame

3/8″ plywood

2x4s

12″x16″ doors

4″ wide face frame

3/4″ plywood shelves

3/8″ plywood

18″x23″ doors

2x4

Beaded board

5 1/2″ face frame

4x4 leg, 34 1/4″ long

2x4

COOK'S DELIGHT

Built of concrete block covered with new brick manufactured to look used, this outdoor kitchen features a gas-fired barbecue and side burners, metal-doored storage cabinets, and a tile countertop. Landscape architects: Ransohoff, Blanchfield, Jones, Inc.

For the outdoor cook who wants to be able to heat a couple of side dishes while attending to the grill, this handsome masonry barbecue has it all. On one side is a commercial-grade, stainless-steel, gas-fired grill; on the other is a matching two-burner cooktop that eliminates the need for trips back and forth to the kitchen.

Harmonizing with the barbecue's used-brick look is a sturdy countertop covered with light, earth-toned ceramic tile. The unglazed tiles and grout are treated with a penetrating sealant to help them repel water and resist stains.

Design Details

This cooking center is basically a large masonry cabinet with two openings on top for drop-in appliance units, and two openings below, with doors, for storage. A reinforced concrete slab supports the structure and forms the floor inside the unit. The walls are actually 6-inch-wide concrete block that were subsequently covered with common brick that is new but manufactured to look used.

Beneath the countertop's tile is a base of 1/2-inch concrete backerboard topped with a 2-inch layer of sand-mix concrete. The counter tiles are mortared onto the dried concrete, and a large backsplash, made with 4-inch bricks and tile, has a flat top that can hold anything from potted plants to plates.

The barbecue and cooktop are both high-end stainless-steel models that will offer years of reliable use and easy cleanup. Both are hooked up to a natural gas line, though propane could be used. (This is not true of all appliances, so check with your dealer.) Centered below each appliance are prehung stainless-steel double doors that fit into openings in the masonry base.

Although the barbecue and cooktop, with precise installation, will seal out rainwater, the doors may not. If your barbecue will get battered by heavy rains, consult with or hire a plumber to install a floor drain in the concrete slab beneath the unit.

Building Notes

Building this barbecue requires skills in masonry and tile work, as well as installing electrical, gas, and plumbing lines. No single task is particularly difficult, but if you lack experience in any of these areas, you may want to contract out some of the work.

Before you begin work, buy the cooking units and doors, which you should be able to find at a barbecue specialty shop or a full-range appliance store. Find out the sizes for all the rough openings and draw your plans carefully to be sure everything will fit exactly. When figuring the openings for the cooking units, don't forget to take into account the total thickness of the countertop: the backerboard, plus the 2 inches of concrete, plus the thickness of the tiles. Make sure to have the units on-site when you build so you can check their fit.

Show your plan to a tile dealer to calculate the amount you will need, and buy only tiles made specifically for countertops. Be sure that all exposed tile edges are "bullnose," with a curved, finished surface. This countertop is made up of four types of tiles: standard field tiles for most of the surface; full-size bullnose pieces for the top of the backsplash; narrow bullnose pieces for the front edges of the top; and corner pieces, or "down angles," for the corners.

MATERIALS CHECKLIST
Gas grill
Gas two-burner outdoor cooktop
Prehung stainless-steel double doors
Gas pipe, shutoff valve, & connections
Electrical conduit, cable, boxes, & GFCI receptacles
Ready-mix concrete (or concrete ingredients)
Lumber & plywood or scrap for concrete forms
3/8" steel reinforcing bar
Concrete blocks
Mortar mix for concrete block
3"x3" angle iron
Common brick
Sand-mix concrete
Masonry screws
1/2-inch concrete backerboard
Thin-set mortar (for surface tile)
Countertop tile
Stain-resistant grout for tile
Silicone caulk

1 Excavate and pour a reinforced concrete slab (see page 110). The perimeter footing of the unit shown is 8 inches wide and 2 feet deep. Don't forget to rough-in gas and electrical lines first.

2 When the slab has cured, lay out and set concrete blocks (see page 120), making sure to provide an opening for the gas pipe. The block forms full walls on three sides and a partial wall on the front side. Working in sections of about 4 square feet, spread mortar onto the blocks and lay a brick wall against the mortared block, working from the bottom up. (See more about working with brick starting on page 114.) Measure precisely so that the cooking units and doors will fit exactly. Over the door openings, install angle irons and lay bricks on top of them. Strike and clean the joints as you go.

3 On the roughed-in gas line, install a T fitting and nipples so gas will be provided to both units. Add shutoff valves and flexible connectors that can reach the cooking units.

4 Install the door units, drilling holes and driving masonry screws to anchor the frames to the brick.

5 Cut pieces of 1/2-inch concrete backerboard for the countertop base so that their edges extend to the outside of the brick walls. Set them in place, measuring to make sure that the cooking units will fit. Be careful not to put too much weight on the backerboard sections or they may break.

6 Trowel a layer of mortar onto the top of the blocks and bricks, and lay the backerboard on top. Temporarily support the backerboard from underneath with 2 by 4s propped in place to keep it from sagging. Use pieces of 2 by 4 to form straight edges. Make a stiff batch of sand-mix concrete and cast a 2-inch-thick slab on top of the concrete board. Trowel the surface smooth. For more about casting concrete, see page 107.

7 When the concrete has cured, remove the temporary supports and forms. Then set the tiles (see page 127). First, lay the tiles in a dry run. You may be able to minimize cuts by widening or narrowing the joints. Use bullnose tiles on the front and side edges and on the backsplash. Once you are sure all the tiles will fit, pick up a section and lay them, then do another section. Use latex-reinforced thin-set mortar and apply with a 1/4-inch-by-1/4-inch notched trowel. After about half the tiles are laid, place a 2 by 6 on top and tap with a hammer to make sure the surface is even.

8 After allowing the mortar to dry at least 24 hours, mix and apply grout (see page 128). Work carefully to produce grout lines that are uniform in appearance. Wipe and rinse with a damp sponge several times as you go. Allow the grout to dry, then buff the surface with a dry towel.

9 Set the cooking units into the openings. To seal out rainwater, run a bead of silicone caulk under the flanges. Connect the flexible gas lines, and test.

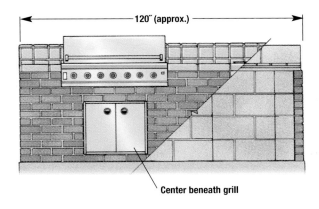

120″ (approx.)

Center beneath grill

Note: Be sure to adapt dimensions to fit your appliances.

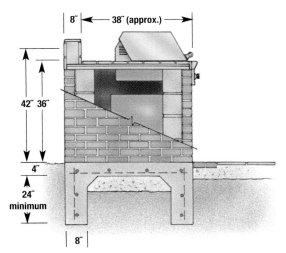

8″ 38″ (approx.)

42″ 36″

4″

24″ minimum

8″

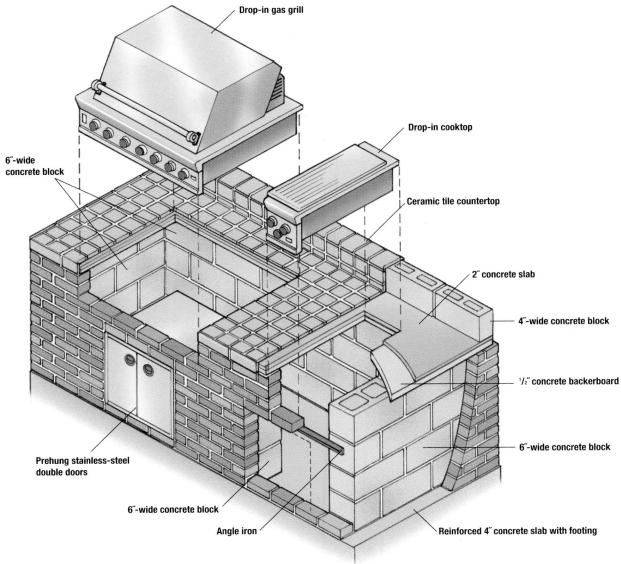

Drop-in gas grill

Drop-in cooktop

6″-wide concrete block

Ceramic tile countertop

2″ concrete slab

4″-wide concrete block

¹/₂″ concrete backerboard

6″-wide concrete block

Prehung stainless-steel double doors

6″-wide concrete block

Angle iron

Reinforced 4″ concrete slab with footing

ELEGANT BARBECUE COUNTER

This handsome granite island has it all—a barbecue, extra burner, and sink in a durable metal construction.
Landscape architects: Truxell & Valentino Landscape Development Inc.
Designer: Phil Kawaguchi, Stone Grove

The first thing you notice about this outdoor cooking island is the stunning backsplash, made of dramatically curved granite. The countertop too is solid granite, a material that is both opulent and practical—it is nearly impossible to stain and wipes up in a flash. Granite also makes for a particularly handsome contrast to the stainless steel of the appliances and cabinet doors.

Neighbors have commented on a subtler feature of this island. While many masonry structures are irregularly shaped, this cabinet has straight, crisp lines and tight corners. The reason: It was framed with metal studs rather than bricks or blocks.

Design Details

The outside of the structure is covered with two layers of stucco. The gap behind the top of the backsplash is filled with mortar, then stuccoed and painted to match the base.

A large professional-quality barbecue resides near the middle of the cabinet, flanked by a burner unit and a sink. The sink rests on top of the countertop so it requires no framing.

Building Notes

Because the cabinet is made of metal studs rather than bricks or block, the concrete slab need not be as massive as for a masonry barbecue. Still, it should be at least 3 inches deep and reinforced with steel; check local codes. A gas line, electrical conduit, water-supply pipes, and a drainpipe all run through the concrete slab and come up inside the cabinet space. The drain line may be connected to the house's main drain, or codes may allow you to run it into a dry well (a large hole filled with gravel).

The metal framing is complicated, so this one was fabricated in a shop and then brought to the site. The cabinet features a 4-inch-by-4-inch toe space at the bottom, just like kitchen cabinets, which makes it easier to stand close to the counter. The shelves that the barbecue unit and side burner rest on are made of steel framing and concrete backerboard.

The entire structure is clad with concrete backerboard screwed onto the metal framing. Corner bead is attached to the outside corners. Two identically curved pieces of backerboard sandwich the steel framing of the backsplash, which was wired for two low-voltage lights during the framing.

1 Pour the concrete foundation after roughing-in electrical, gas, and plumbing lines. See page 110 for information on casting a slab. The slab should be strengthened with $^1/_2$-inch steel reinforcing bar,

This secondary gas burner allows cooking side dishes while the main course barbecues on the grill.

MATERIALS LIST

Gas grill & side burner

Prehung stainless-steel doors

Stainless-steel sink, faucet, & plumbing

Gas pipe, shutoff valve, & connections

Electrical conduit, cable, boxes, & GFCI receptacles

Two exterior low-voltage lights

Floor drain and PVC drainpipe

Ready-mix concrete (or concrete ingredients)

Lumber & plywood or scrap for concrete forms

$^1/_2$″ steel reinforcing bar

Steel studs & channels

$^1/_2$″ concrete backerboard

Sheet-metal screws

Fiberglass mesh

Thin-set mortar

Stucco corner bead

Sand stucco mix

crisscrossed and spaced every 12 inches. To cut the steel bar, use a metal-cutting blade mounted on a power circular saw. Be sure to wear safety glasses and gloves.

2 Purchase the barbecue and burner units, and build the steel framing to accommodate them. Pay close attention to the dimensions of the openings, and don't forget to take into account the backerboard's $1/2$-inch thickness. The barbecue unit is heavy, so be sure it will be supported with framing, not just backerboard.

3 The framing is complicated, but working with metal studs is a manageable job. There are two types of metal framing members, both of them U-shaped—channels (also called tracks), and studs, which fit into the channels. Use channels for most of the horizontal members and studs for most of the vertical members. Cut the pieces to length with a pair of tin snips. Once two pieces have been joined together, drive sheet-metal screws specially designed for metal studs into the flanges on either side.

4 When turning a corner with channel, snip the flanges and fold them out. If you need to join a horizontal channel somewhere in the middle of a stud, cut and bend back about 3 inches of the channel and slip it onto the stud. For more about working with steel studs, refer to the directions for the project that begins on page 38.

5 To make the substrate for the curved backsplash, run the studs up longer than

they will ultimately be. Make a cardboard template and cut backerboard in the shape of the backsplash (it will take two pieces to form the complete curve).

6 Set the backerboard in place against the studs and mark each stud for cutting—1 inch shorter than the top of the backerboard. Cut pieces of channel to fit between the studs and install them more than 1 inch below the top of the curved backerboard.

7 Use the template to cut backerboard pieces for the back of the unit. Attach the backerboard in front and in back with sheet-metal screws. Cut strips of backerboard to fit between the two "sandwich" pieces, and anchor them with screws.

8 Fill the channel with mortar. When you reach the top, apply fiberglass mesh to the joints and cover it with a finish coat of thin-set mortar to create a smooth curve.

9 Cut pieces of concrete backerboard and join them to the framing with special screws. Attach stucco corner bead to all outside corners. Apply stucco in two coats—a scratch coat and a finish coat (see page 119)—to all surfaces that will be exposed.

10 Have a granite company cut and install a granite top and backsplash to fit. Put in the barbecue and burner units (see page 131). Set the sink into the countertop, install the faucet, and hook up the plumbing (see page 132). Finally, complete the electrical wiring (see page 136).

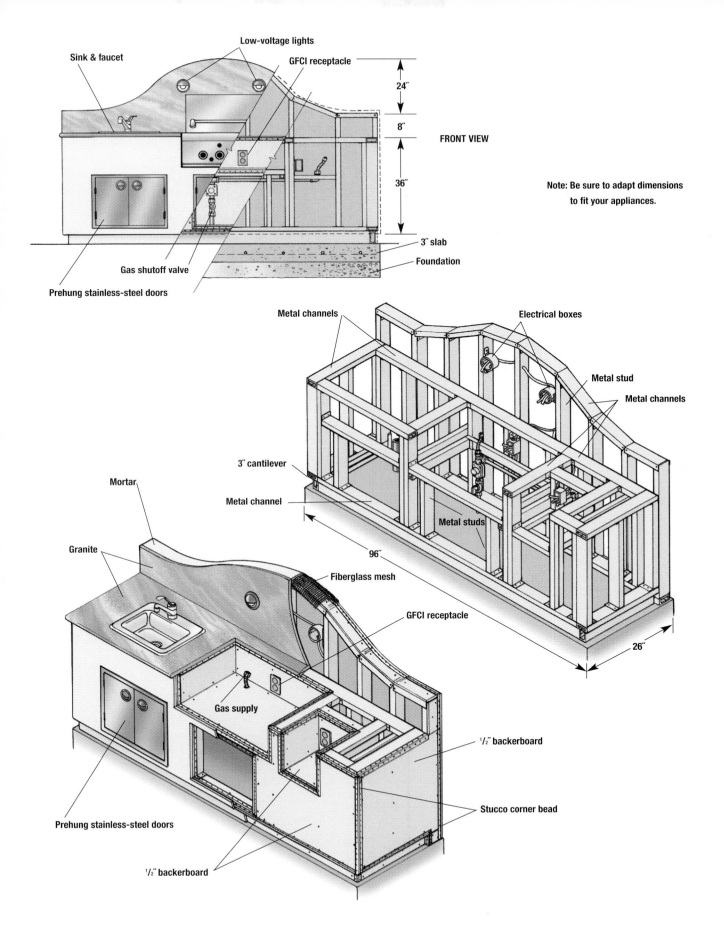

Sink & faucet

Low-voltage lights

GFCI receptacle

24″

8″

FRONT VIEW

36″

Note: Be sure to adapt dimensions
to fit your appliances.

3″ slab

Foundation

Gas shutoff valve

Prehung stainless-steel doors

Metal channels

Electrical boxes

Metal stud

Metal channels

3″ cantilever

Metal channel

Metal studs

96″

Mortar

Granite

Fiberglass mesh

GFCI receptacle

26″

Gas supply

1/2″ backerboard

Prehung stainless-steel doors

1/2″ backerboard

Stucco corner bead

L-SHAPED BARBECUE

This comprehensive outdoor kitchen turns a corner with a broad serving counter.
Landscape designers: Christopher Lines Landscape Design & Consultation

Neatly fitted into a corner of the patio, this comfortably sized outdoor kitchen is designed to expand the home out to the backyard for year-round dining and entertaining. A full-featured cooking center, it has a gas grill, side burner, sink, refrigerator, and three storage cabinets with stainless-steel doors. The unit's L shape provides ample and easily proximity counter space for food preparation; its adjacency to the house greatly eases the tasks of hooking up to gas, plumbing, and electrical lines.

Design Details

Though it appears to be built of used brick, the basic structure is actually concrete block that has been surfaced with a used-brick veneer (newly manufactured half-thickness bricks that are made to look used). The glazed ceramic tile on the countertop is laid over a base of pressure-treated exterior-grade plywood that is held back 2 inches from the grill and side burner as a required fire-safety measure.

Building Notes

The dimensions and form of this unit can be easily adjusted to suit most any backyard. If you decide to build it, try to set the dimensions of the structural concrete-block base so that it requires only standard 8-by-8-by-16-inch concrete blocks. Be sure to have the grill and other appliances on-site before construction begins so you can verify their fit as you work.

1 Lay out the L-shaped base and, if you're not building it on top of an existing slab, cast the concrete footing and slab as discussed on page 110. Refer to the illustrations on page 60 for specific dimensions. If any plumbing or conduit must penetrate the slab, be sure to place it before pouring the concrete.

2 Begin building the base from concrete block, as discussed on page 120. Place a $1/2$-inch reinforcing bar vertically in the block cores every 16 inches and lay one horizontally across every other course.

3 As you build the block walls, leave openings for the cabinet doors and appliances, per the specifications of the manufacturers. Bridge across the tops of the openings with angle iron, as shown in the sidebar on page 118.

4 Once you've built the entire concrete-block base, add the brick veneer. Working in areas of approximately 4 square feet at a time, apply a coat of mortar to the faces of the concrete blocks. Lay a bed of mortar for the bricks (see page 113), coat the back edge of each brick with a thin layer of mortar, and place the bricks against the blocks. Start at the bottom corners and work toward the centers of each wall.

The counter to the right of the barbecue grill caps an outdoor refrigerator and a storage cabinet.

MATERIALS CHECKLIST

Gas grill with side burner

Prehung stainless-steel doors

Stainless-steel sink, faucet & plumbing

Below-counter exterior refrigerator

Gas pipe, shutoff valve, & connections

Electrical conduit, cable, boxes, & GFCI receptacles

Ready-mix concrete (or concrete ingredients)

Lumber & plywood or scrap for concrete forms

$1/2″$ steel reinforcing bar

Concrete blocks

Used brick veneer

Mortar mix for concrete block

Mortar mix for brick

3″ x3″ angle iron

Steel studs (or other counter support framing)

Pressure-treated exterior-grade plywood

Thin-set mortar (for surface tile)

Countertop tile

Tile spacers

Stain-resistant grout for tile

Grout sealer

Various masonry screws & concrete nails

5 You can build the countertop using any of several methods. To provide a sturdy base for it, you'll need to install some type of support framing across the top of the concrete blocks—either steel or wood. For a complete discussion of countertop building techniques, see page 124. If you install a plywood countertop base, be sure to hold it back from the grill and side burner at least 2 inches (more if required by the grill manufacturer). Before you actually tile the countertop, be sure to accurately figure the sink and grill installations (you may need to install the sink first if it is not self-rimming).

6 Install the plumbing for the sink and the gas-supply connections as discussed on pages 132–135. Also install the electrical wiring for the refrigerator and any electrical outlets, making sure to use ground-fault circuit interrupter (GFCI) receptacles. See page 136 for more about hooking up wiring.

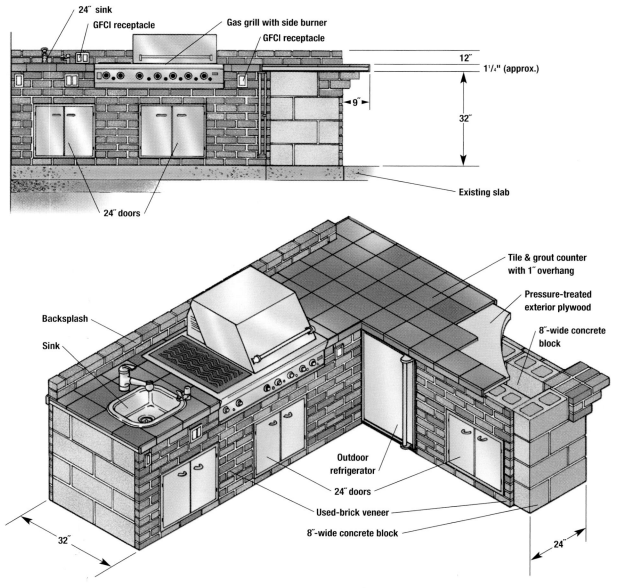

24″ sink
GFCI receptacle
Gas grill with side burner
GFCI receptacle
12″
1¹/₄″ (approx.)
9″
32″
Existing slab
24″ doors

Backsplash
Sink
Tile & grout counter with 1″ overhang
Pressure-treated exterior plywood
8″-wide concrete block
Outdoor refrigerator
24″ doors
Used-brick veneer
8″-wide concrete block
32″
24″

SUNSET CLASSIC: SIMPLE BRICK BARBECUE

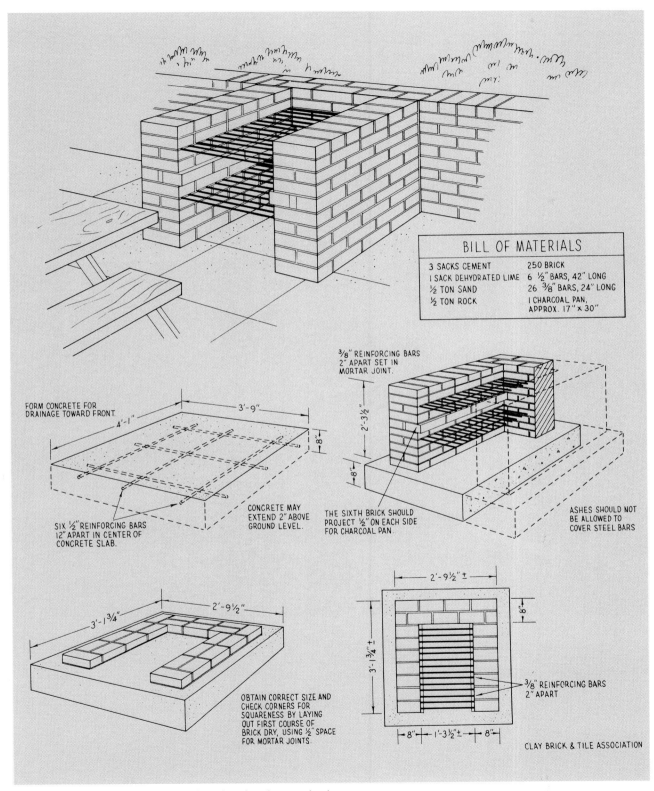

BILL OF MATERIALS

3 SACKS CEMENT	250 BRICK
1 SACK DEHYDRATED LIME	6 ½" BARS, 42" LONG
½ TON SAND	26 ⅜" BARS, 24" LONG
½ TON ROCK	1 CHARCOAL PAN, APPROX. 17" x 30"

FORM CONCRETE FOR DRAINAGE TOWARD FRONT.

4'-1"

3'-9"

8"

SIX ½" REINFORCING BARS 12" APART IN CENTER OF CONCRETE SLAB.

CONCRETE MAY EXTEND 2" ABOVE GROUND LEVEL.

⅜" REINFORCING BARS 2" APART SET IN MORTAR JOINT.

2'-3½"

8"

THE SIXTH BRICK SHOULD PROJECT ½" ON EACH SIDE FOR CHARCOAL PAN.

ASHES SHOULD NOT BE ALLOWED TO COVER STEEL BARS

3'-1¾"

2'-9½"

OBTAIN CORRECT SIZE AND CHECK CORNERS FOR SQUARENESS BY LAYING OUT FIRST COURSE OF BRICK DRY, USING ½" SPACE FOR MORTAR JOINTS.

2'-9½" ±

8"

3'-1¾" ±

⅜" REINFORCING BARS 2" APART

8" — 1'-3½" ± — 8"

CLAY BRICK & TILE ASSOCIATION

Some barbecues are timeless. The design shown here, based on a project in "The Sunset Barbecue Book," published in 1946, first appeared in "Sunset Ideas for Building Barbecues" in 1950.

FULL-FEATURED OUTDOOR KITCHEN

Slate walls and a porcelain-tile counter combine to
make this striking L-shaped outdoor kitchen.
Landscape architects: Michael Glassman & Associates
Mason: Jeff Nelms, Nelm's Construction

A generous gas grill, side burners, corner sink, refrigerator, and storage cabinets make this cooking center a dream come true for the outdoor chef. The porcelain-tile counter is both beautiful and hardworking, offering a durable, broad surface for meal preparation, serving, and dining. The slate walls of the barbecue blend harmoniously with the slate patio.

Design Details

Beneath the barbecue's slate walls is a sturdy masonry structure built of concrete block. A solid reinforced-concrete foundation supports the heavy structure and a concrete slab at the top of the unit offers a flat, non-combustible substrate for the countertop tile.

Opposite the work area, the counter has a broad overhang to provide a comfortable eating counter. Because the homeowners are tall, this barbecue is 40 inches high rather than the typical 36 inches—though you can easily alter the design to suit your needs.

The barbecue grill, side burner, sink, refrigerator, and storage doors are all made from stainless steel for durable, reliable use and easy cleanup. Both the barbecue and side burner are hooked up to a gas line. The stainless-steel doors are mounted to the masonry and provide access to the gas shutoff valves and plumbing connections as well as to storage space.

Building Notes

Before you begin construction, buy the appliances and cabinet doors and refer to the owner's manuals for proper rough-in sizes. Because many cuts must be made in both the slate and porcelain tile, it's a good idea to rent a "wet" tile-cutting saw with a diamond blade.

1 Excavate and install forms for a reinforced concrete foundation. The unit shown has a 12-by-12-inch perimeter footing; another option is to pour a 6-inch-thick concrete slab for the unit.

2 Strengthen the footing with $1/2$-inch reinforcing bars placed horizontally on 12-inch centers. If you opt for a slab foundation, place reinforcing bars in a grid pattern every 12 inches. Support them about 3 inches off the ground with small pieces of broken concrete blocks or brick. Cut the reinforcing bar with a steel-cutting blade mounted on a circular saw (be sure to wear gloves and safety glasses).

3 Have a plumber rough-in a gas line as well as water supplies and drain a for the sink, according to the plans. The gas pipe should be located where its valve can be easily accessed. Decide where you want electrical receptacles and be sure the conduit is stubbed-up where it can run through the concrete-block cells. Mount the water supplies and drain beneath the sink's location. Cast the foundation, as discussed on page 110.

4 Build the concrete block walls, following the techniques discussed on page 120. Leave openings for the storage doors and refrigerator, and recesses for the grill and side burner. Use angle iron to support the blocks where they bridge openings, as shown on page 118. Scrape excess mortar from the joints as you work (it isn't nec-

MATERIALS CHECKLIST

Gas grill

Gas two-burner outdoor cooktop

Prehung stainless-steel doors

Stainless-steel sink, faucet, & plumbing

Below-counter exterior refrigerator

Gas pipe, shutoff valve, & connections

Electrical conduit, cable, boxes, & GFCI receptacles

Ready-mix concrete (or concrete ingredients)

Lumber & plywood or scrap for concrete forms

$1/8$" hardboard for concrete forms

$1/2$" & $3/8$" steel reinforcing bar

Concrete blocks

Mortar mix for concrete block

Slate tile

Mortar mix (for slate)

Porcelain tile

Thin-set mortar (for surface tile)

Tile spacers

Stain-resistant grout

Tile & stone sealer

essary to strike them because they will be covered by the slate).

5 Reinforce the walls as you build by placing $1/2$-inch steel reinforcing bar vertically in every other cell and running a $3/8$-inch reinforcing bar horizontally along each course. Build four courses of 8-by-8-by-16-inch blocks beneath the cooktop and side burner and five courses for the other walls. When you reach the top course, fill the cells with grout (see page 104), but don't grout cells where electrical conduit is located.

6 Once the grout has set, build the forms for the countertop slab. Start by building a temporary platform inside the blocks out of several pieces of scrap $5/8$- or $3/4$-inch plywood (use pieces so you can remove them from inside the unit after the concrete sets up). Support this platform on temporary 1-by-4 ledgers fastened to the concrete blocks with concrete nails or screws.

7 Add additional 2-by-4 props underneath and stiltlike supports from 2 by 4s along the outer sides of the forms (see detail). Use $1/8$-inch hardboard to form the curved end of the counter. Fasten short pieces of hardboard flush to the blocks in the barbecue area with concrete nails; make a hardboard "fence" that will keep the concrete out of the sink's location.

8 Cut in rectangular holes for waterproof electrical boxes and mount the boxes on the electrical conduit stubbed up through the blocks (see more about this on page

136). To cut these holes, a hand grinder with a masonry-cutting blade is the easiest tool to use.

9 Reinforce the countertop with a crisscrossed grid of $1/2$-inch steel reinforcing bar placed every 12 inches. Support this grid with pieces of broken blocks, about an inch up from the platform. Cast the concrete slab as discussed on page 110 and allow it to cure.

10 Install the slate tile on the walls. Work in 4-square-foot areas at a time. First trowel a layer of mortar onto the blocks and the backs of the slate. Press a piece of slate into position and seat it by tapping gently with a rubber mallet. Work from one bottom corner, moving upward and across the wall.

11 Lay the countertop tile following the methods discussed on page 124. Do a dry run before permanently setting the tiles to minimize cutting by widening or narrowing the joints. After about half the tiles are laid, place a 2 by 6 across the surface and tap with a hammer to seat the tiles and ensure a flat surface.

12 Allow the mortar to dry completely, then mix and apply grout (see page 128). Allow the grout to dry, then buff the surface with a towel.

13 Set the gas grill and side burner into place and hook them up as discussed on page 131. For information on installing the sink, see page 132; to complete the electrical work, see page 136.

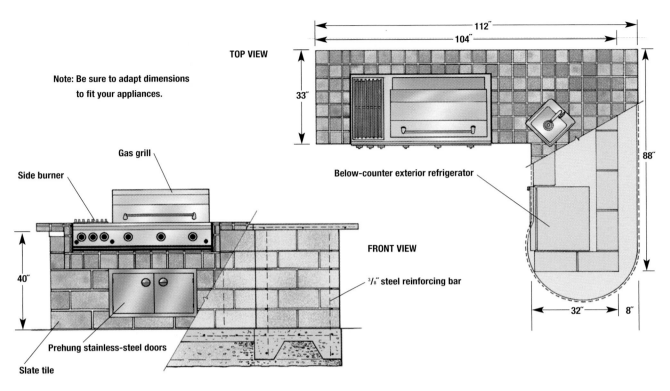

TOP VIEW

112″

104″

33″

88″

32″ 8″

Note: Be sure to adapt dimensions
to fit your appliances.

Gas grill

Side burner

Below-counter exterior refrigerator

FRONT VIEW

³/₈″ steel reinforcing bar

40″

Prehung stainless-steel doors

Slate tile

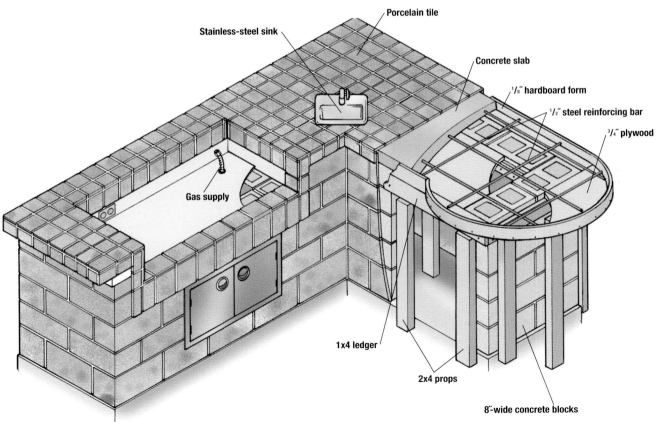

Porcelain tile

Stainless-steel sink

Concrete slab

¹/₈″ hardboard form

¹/₂″ steel reinforcing bar

³/₄″ plywood

Gas supply

1x4 ledger

2x4 props

8″-wide concrete blocks

SCULPTURAL FIRE PIT

Designed to complement the barbecue shown on page
30, this circular gas-fueled fire pit features elegant slate
cladding and a custom-made metal sculpture that serves
as a backdrop and windscreen for the fire.
Landscape architect: David Fox
Fire-screen sculptor: LMNO Arts

The raised rim around this elegant and artful fire pit defines its form, and a wide front section of the rim serves as a comfortable bench. Though crafting a metal sculpture like the one at the center of the fire pit calls for the talents of a metal artisan, building the fire pit itself is a relatively simple job.

Design Details

The fire pit's circular wall is built from 8-by-8-by-8-inch and 4-by-8-by-8-inch concrete blocks covered with a veneer of slate. The narrower 4-inch-wide blocks are used for the back half of the circle, as shown in the illustration on page 69. A log lighter, controlled by a valve at the front of the unit, allows for instantaneous fires. If you prefer a different surface material, such as brick or stone, you can easily modify the design. It's also easy to adjust the fire pit's diameter.

Building Notes

The concrete blocks sit on a continuous concrete footing, and the metal sculpture is supported by a second footing cast in a semicircle just inside the rear wall section. The diameter of the fire pit shown is about 6 feet. It's a good idea to set up the blocks in a circle before starting construction so you can adjust the measurements to minimize or eliminate the need for cutting blocks. Measure the outside diameter of your test circle and divide it by two to figure the exact radius of your fire pit.

Plan to have the metal sculpture finished and on-site before beginning construction so you can verify dimensions for its footing. Also buy the log lighter before starting work and keep it nearby for reference. For cutting the slate, you may want to rent a "wet" tile-

This stucco-based fire pit's shape repeats the patio's rectilinear lines.

cutting saw; otherwise, you can use a circular saw with a masonry-cutting blade. Be sure to wear gloves and safety glasses when cutting.

1   Drive a peg into the center of the fire pit's location and tie a string to it. Measure out from the peg a distance equal to your fire pit's radius, tie a stick to the string, and use the stick to scribe your fire pit's outside circumference on the ground. Pour chalk along this mark or dig straight down with a shovel to set the mark. When digging the trenches, make their walls as vertical as possible; clean out loose dirt, and recheck the circumference occasionally.

2   Excavate to 12 inches below the frost line and make the trenches at least 9 inches wide so the resulting footing will support the block plus the slate (make it wider if you'll be using a brick or stone veneer).

3   Use a circular saw equipped with a metal-cutting blade to cut 1/4-inch steel reinforcing bars to lengths equal to the footing's depth

plus about 20 inches. Pound them perfectly vertically into the ground about 4 inches (so 16 inches will stand above the footings) along the center of the trenches, spaced approximately 16 inches apart, and where they will run through the cell of every other concrete block.

4 Build a form for casting the sculpture's semicircular footing. Use $^1/_8$-inch hardboard to form the curve; temporarily nail it to pointed 2 by 4s driven into the ground and stake it as required to maintain the proper curved shape and make the form sturdy.

5 Cast the concrete footings (see page 107), making sure they are level and flat. Sink copper rods into the sculpture's footing as shown in the upper right illustration on the facing page (later, the sculpture will be brazed to these). Allow the footings to cure for at least three days and keep them damp during that period.

6 Lay the concrete blocks following the directions given on page 120. Because these blocks are laid in a circular pattern, you'll need to butt together their inside corners and pack mortar into the gaps around the outer face. Use a carpenter's level to ensure level from block to block as you work.

7 Have a plumber rough-in a gas line to the pit's location, run the pipe through the blocks, and install the gas valve for the log lighter. If you run the pipe next to the blocks, as shown in the illustration at top right on the facing page, be sure it is

buried in the sand as shown. Be sure the valve is turned off before work starts, and protect the valve and log lighter's connection point by wrapping the ends with duct tape.

8 Fill the cells of the concrete blocks with a very loose, gravel-free mixture of concrete and, using a trowel, pack it, then scrape the surface smooth.

9 Lay out the slate pieces in an attractive arrangement. Mix mortar, then, working from the bottom up, spread it on the face of the concrete blocks. Butter the back of each piece of slate, then press the slate onto the blocks. Use plastic tile spacers to hold the bottom course of slate off the ground and to maintain even grout lines. Immediately wipe excess mortar off the face of the slate.

10 Allow the mortar to dry completely, then mix up grout for the slate. Apply the stain-resistant grout as discussed on page 130. Allow it to dry, then apply a grout sealer according to directions on the sealer package.

11 Fill the area inside the fire pit with gravel to within about 6 inches of the top. Add another 3 inches of coarse sand, then install the gas-log assembly and hook it up to the log lighter as directed by the manufacturer. If you're not familiar with doing this type of installation, contract the services of a plumber.

12 Finally, have the metal sculpture brazed onto the copper rods by a professional.

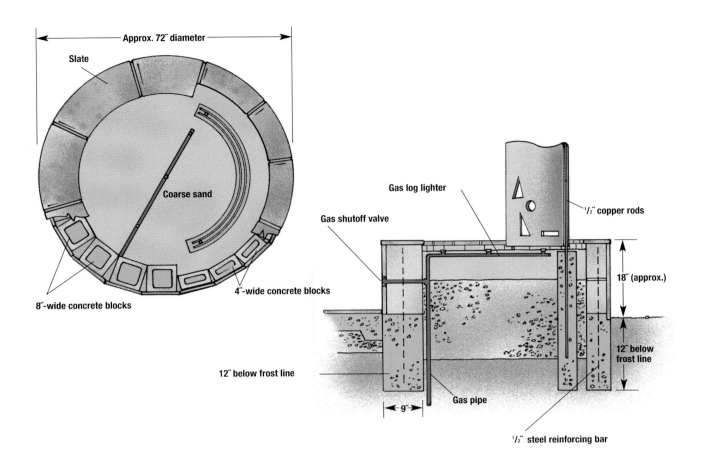

Approx. 72″ diameter

Slate

Coarse sand

8″-wide concrete blocks

4″-wide concrete blocks

Gas log lighter

Gas shutoff valve

½″ copper rods

18″ (approx.)

12″ below frost line

12″ below frost line

Gas pipe

9″

½″ steel reinforcing bar

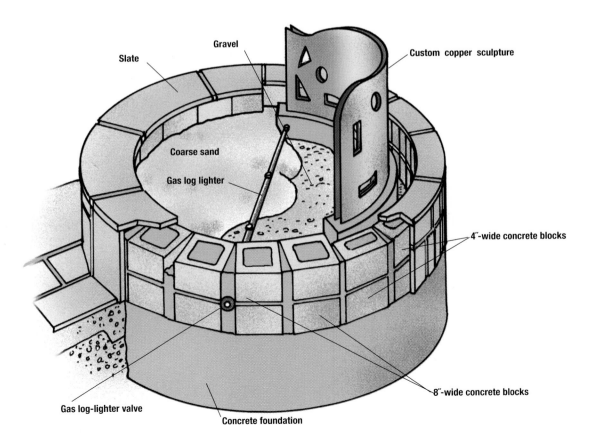

Slate

Gravel

Custom copper sculpture

Coarse sand

Gas log lighter

4″-wide concrete blocks

8″-wide concrete blocks

Gas log-lighter valve

Concrete foundation

ADOBE OVEN

This simple adobe oven can be constructed in a matter
of days and is great for cooking pizzas, roasts, vegeta-
bles, and crusty loaves of bread.
Designer and builder: Peter O. Whiteley

This adobe oven is modeled after mud-brick ovens used around the world, from Mexico, Italy, and France to the Southwestern United States. It is an efficient means to all sorts of wood-fired cooking.

Design Details

The project takes only about two days of work; it speeds up building to have two or three people making the thick-walled adobe shell, the mass of which stores the heat of the fire.

Building Notes

Find a safe, level location in your garden for the oven, a safe distance away from any combustible surface, such as a fence or decking. Also, check with local officials about property line setback requirements.

The oven shown here was built on a 6-by-8-foot base of red concrete steppingstones—an optional part of the project. The rest of the base is stacked but mortarless, which allows for easy disassembly if desired in the future.

You'll find most of the materials you need at a home improvement center or building supply yard, except for the cardboard barrel, which is used to form the oven's curving top. (Look in the telephone book under *Barrels & Drums*).

You'll also need a tape measure, hacksaw, pencil, circular saw with masonry bit, wire cutters, saber saw, drill, screwdriver, large wheelbarrow, hoe, shovel, sturdy rubber gloves, sponge, small piece of scrap lumber or plywood, old towels, and plastic tarp.

1 Arrange the 8-by-8-by-16-inch concrete blocks on the ground to make a 32-by-54-inch base. Cover the base with an

identical layout of cap blocks. Then add a layer of firebricks.

2 Cut the barrel in half lengthwise with a hacksaw. Center an empty quart can on the closed end of one half-barrel; trace and cut out its circular shape for the vent.

3 Score and cut two firebricks in half with a circular saw (halves measure $4^{1}/_{2}$ inches square). For more brick-cutting techniques, see page 114.

4 Starting at the back end of the base, make three U-shaped layers of firebricks to support the half-barrel. Each layer is three bricks long and $2^{1}/_{2}$ bricks wide at the back end. Position the barrel on the bricks, as shown above.

5 Cut a 3-by-4-foot piece of the 6-inch wire mesh and shape it so it arcs over the barrel by about 1 inch. Bend and tuck any excess under the bricks at the side. Then cover the 6-inch wire mesh with at least one layer of chicken wire, bending and

MATERIALS CHECKLIST

14 concrete building blocks (8˝x8˝x16˝)

14 concrete cap blocks (8˝x2˝x16˝)

68 firebricks ($2^{1}/_{2}$˝x$4^{1}/_{2}$˝x9˝)

1 cardboard barrel, 28 to 30 gallons

1 empty 1-quart can

6´ square of 6˝ wire mesh

10´ of 30˝-wide chicken wire

4´ of rough-sawn redwood 2x4

2´ of redwood 1x3

16 1$^{1}/_{2}$˝ deck screws

3´ of 6˝-wide aluminum flashing

8 large wheelbarrow loads of adobe soil

3 bags portland cement

1´ square of $^{1}/_{4}$˝ galvanized wire mesh (see sidebar)

Exterior latex paint

24 precast 1´x2´ concrete steppingstones (optional)

folding the edges over the rear and open end of the barrel in a similar manner.

6 Make the door shown on the facing page. Cut three 14-inch-long pieces from redwood 2-by-4 lumber. Join them together with screws running through two parallel lengths of 1-by-3 redwood across the front. Cut the top into an arch that measures 14 inches tall at the peak and conforms to the basic shape of the open end of the barrel. Shape the handle from excess 2-by-4 redwood, and attach it to the 1 by 3s with screws. Center and tack flashing around the door's perimeter. Insert the can in the hole cut in the rear of the barrel.

7 Mix three parts adobe soil to one part portland cement, add water, and mix with a hoe and shovel to the consistency of thick oatmeal. Be forewarned: this is tiring and muddy work. Test that the mix holds together by squeezing it.

8 Working from the base up, pack the adobe-cement mixture firmly over and through the layers of mesh, making sure there are no air pockets. Pack the mixture around the can, wiggling and rotating the

can to keep it from being trapped in place. Form the arch for the door by squeezing the mixture into the chicken wire, and periodically inserting the door (with flashing attached) to check the fit. Continue adding mixture until the coat is 4 to 5 inches thick overall. Let it dry slightly, then smooth the surface with a damp sponge and a wood float made with scrap lumber.

9 Wiggle the door and can, then cover the oven with damp towels and a plastic tarp. Keep the towels damp and the oven covered for at least a week while the adobe hardens and cures. Remove the flashing from the door.

10 Paint the adobe shell after building the first fire, if desired.

11 To build a first fire in the oven, remove the can from the rear vent and cut and fit a piece of $1/4$-inch wire mesh over the vent to act as a spark arrester. Build a small fire and keep it burning steadily so the adobe warms slowly and any remaining moisture is baked out. Hairline cracks will likely develop, but they can be sealed with coats of exterior latex paint.

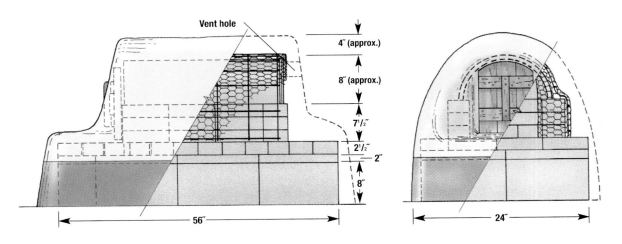

Vent hole

4″ (approx.)

8″ (approx.)

7¹⁄₂″

2¹⁄₂″

2″

8″

56″

24″

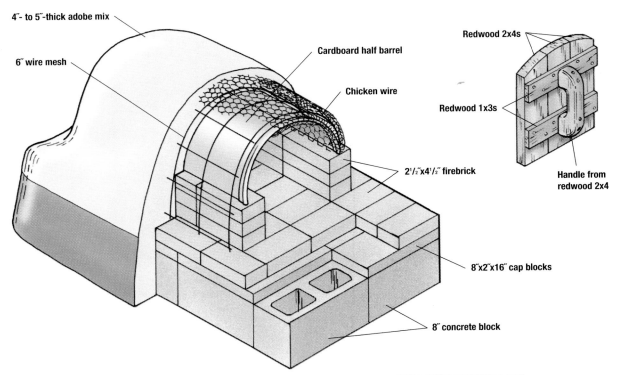

4″- to 5″-thick adobe mix

6″ wire mesh

Cardboard half barrel

Chicken wire

Redwood 2x4s

Redwood 1x3s

Handle from redwood 2x4

2¹⁄₂″x4¹⁄₂″ firebrick

8″x2″x16″ cap blocks

8″ concrete block

HEATING AND COOKING IN THE OVEN

After the first fire, follow these directions for heating and cooking:

0 to 10 minutes: Screen the vent and open the door. In the center of the oven, mound six to eight sheets of crumpled newspaper. Lean two or three handfuls of kindling wood, including some 1-inch-thick pieces, teepee-style against the paper. Ignite the paper, and when the kindling is burning well, lay two or three more handfuls of kindling on the fire and top it with three or four logs 3 to 4 inches thick and about 1¹⁄₂ feet long.

20 to 40 minutes: When the logs begin to burn, add six more logs, 4 to 5 inches thick, but be careful of heat from the oven door—it can singe hair. Toss about half of a 10-pound bag of charcoal briquettes between the logs. Let the fire burn about one hour, then add the remaining briquettes. Burn until most of the wood is gone, about three hours total. Occasionally poke the fire to keep air circulating.

At about 2 hours and 50 minutes: With a shovel, scoop the hot ashes into a fireproof metal container partially filled with water. Quickly clean the oven floor with a wet mop or wet towel tied to a pole.

2 hours and 50 minutes to 3 hours: Set an oven thermometer on the floor just inside the door. Close the door and block the vent. Check after 10 minutes. The temperature should be between 700° and 650° but will quickly drop to 600°.

The next four hours, bake.

CHIMNEY COOKER

If entertaining on a big scale is your style, a smoker may be the best choice for your outdoor cooking center. Landscape architects: Irvine's Design

Though it does not require an extensive amount of space, this Chinese-style cooker/smoker can handle up to 10 chickens, roasts, or whole fish at a time. Because it circulates intense, smoky heat around whatever is being cooked, there is no need to turn the food, and you end up with meat, fish, or fowl that is juicy yet drained of excess fat.

The heart of the system, the chimney, is simplicity itself—a cylindrical concrete drainpipe, about 2 feet in diameter and 4 feet tall. A square hole cut in the bottom of the drainpipe and positioned next to an adjacent fire pit allows smoke and heat from the fire to enter the chimney. You control the heat by moving the fire nearer to or farther from the chimney's hole, and also by opening or closing a metal lid atop the chimney.

Design Details

The structure shown on the facing page is part of a patio surface and a connecting section with a drop-in barbecue unit. For this project, we concentrate on the fire pit and the chimney.

A thick, reinforced concrete slab is needed to support the chimney's massive weight (see page 110 for information on casting a slab). The fire pit, which also rests on the concrete slab, is made of standard brick, with a firebrick facing on the inside.

The brickwork is tricky, so hire a mason if you do not have experience. Because they go around tight curves, the bricks must be bevel-cut to one-third length—longer bricks would create a very uneven surface. It's necessary to bevel-cut the pieces to maintain even mortar joints. To accomplish this

This tower-like structure is another approach to the smoker. Here, custom metalwork brings classic styling to the outdoor cooking center.
Design: City Building Inc.

work, rent a masonry-cutting saw. Be sure to wear safety glasses when cutting brick.

Building Notes

To simplify construction considerably, you may choose not to face the chimney with bricks; the concrete tube is plenty thick without them. If you don't like the look of the raw concrete, you can stucco the concrete's exterior (see page 119).

Another alternative: Replace the concrete drainpipe with one made of reddish-brown terra cotta, which is nearly as heavy as a concrete pipe but is easier to cut and has a more pleasing appearance. Because it is not steel-reinforced, be sure to handle it with care or it may crack or break.

Yet another option is to construct a standard chimney by stacking sections of square chimney liner and building a brick facing around it. See page 114 for information on building with brick.

To build a unit like the one shown at left, first locate a section of steel-reinforced concrete drainpipe, about 3 inches thick and 22

MATERIALS CHECKLIST
3″-thick concrete drainpipe, 54″ long x 22″ diameter
Ready-mix concrete (or concrete ingredients)
$1/2$″ steel reinforcing bar
Benderboard & stakes
Common bricks
Mortar mix for brick
Firebricks
Refractory mortar
Custom metal support shelf
Custom metal lid

inches in diameter. A sewer supply source may sell you one. Or, you might be able to scavenge one from a salvage yard (similar drainpipes are used in parks as playground equipment).

Then, you must solve two logistical problems: cutting and moving the pipe. First, decide how you want to cut it. Doing this yourself will be difficult—you'll need to rent a diamond-bladed saw large enough for the job. Better yet, pay the supplier to cut it for you. Cut the pipe to 54 inches in length. At one end, cut out a 12-by-12-inch opening.

The second logistical problem is moving and placing the concrete chimney, which will weigh about 800 pounds. You will probably need several helpers, a come-along, and a heavy-duty pickup truck. Again, you're better off requesting delivery by the supplier and having them send along a forklift.

Have a sheet-metal shop manufacture two heavy steel parts for you: a curved, flat shelf to support the bricks over the opening between the chimney and the fire pit, and a lid with a handle for the chimney.

1   Excavate and construct forms for a 6-inch-deep concrete pad in a sort of figure-eight pattern (see the upper right-hand illustration on the facing page). The smaller circular portion should be about 6 inches larger in diameter than the concrete drainpipe. Pour the concrete (see page 107), and set in pieces of $1/2$-inch steel reinforcing bar, crisscrossed on 12-inch centers. Allow the slab to cure for four or five days.

2   Place the drainpipe on top of the slab; because of its weight, it isn't necessary to mortar it in place. Make sure the opening at the bottom of the drainpipe faces the fire pit.

3   About 6 inches from the top, drill four $1/2$-inch holes in the chimney, and slide in two pieces of $1/2$-inch reinforcing bar, as shown in the lower right-hand illustration on the facing page.

4   Cut five or six bricks for the chimney section (with $3/4$-inch bevels) and five or six for the firebox, and lay them in a dry run to test whether the bevels are correct. Cut each brick in thirds with bevel cuts as shown below near right. To achieve even mortar lines, you may need to adjust the angle of the cuts.

5   See page 114 for general instructions on laying bricks. Facing a curved section is tricky, because you cannot string a line to check for level. Spread mortar onto the cylinder, no more than 4 square feet at a time, and press the bricks into it. Every few bricks, measure up from the concrete slab and check with a level to make sure you are maintaining level and straight lines. Strike and clean joints as you go.

6   To build the fire pit, lay the first course of bricks in a mortar bed, then add the remaining two courses. Cut and lay firebricks to line the inside of the fire pit (see illustration at right), placing them on end. Cut cap bricks lengthwise using the same angle as you used for the bricks below, and lay them on top. Strike and clean the bricks.

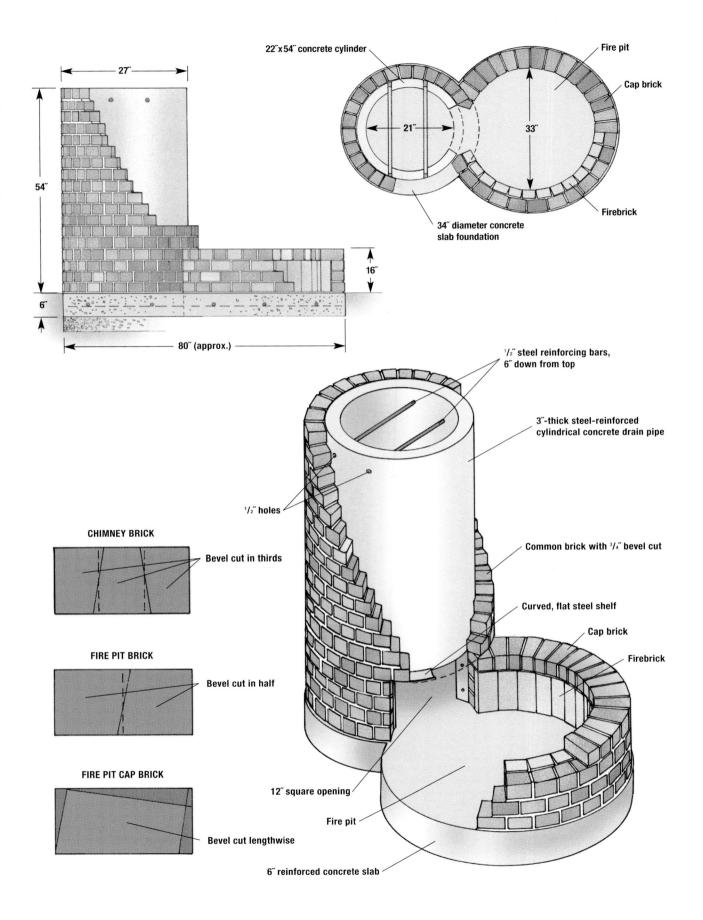

27″

54″

6″

16″

80″ (approx.)

22″x54″ concrete cylinder

Fire pit

Cap brick

21″

33″

Firebrick

34″ diameter concrete
slab foundation

½″ steel reinforcing bars,
6″ down from top

3″-thick steel-reinforced
cylindrical concrete drain pipe

½″ holes

Common brick with ¾″ bevel cut

Curved, flat steel shelf

Cap brick

Firebrick

CHIMNEY BRICK

Bevel cut in thirds

FIRE PIT BRICK

Bevel cut in half

FIRE PIT CAP BRICK

Bevel cut lengthwise

12″ square opening

Fire pit

6″ reinforced concrete slab

COLORFUL CONTEMPORARY

This stylish barbecue, featured on the cover, is a
delightful center of attraction for a contemporary
outdoor entertaining area.
Landscape architects: Michael Glassman & Associates

A sea of blue ceramic tile sweeps across this curved barbecue island, elegantly blending the unit with the home's contemporary style. Below the tile counter, yellow, sandy-toned stucco walls provide a simple yet colorful base. Centered in the counter, a large gas-fueled grill offers enough firepower for entertaining large groups.

Design Details

The unit is actually built of concrete blocks that have been given a finish coat of stucco. Underneath the tile counter a reinforced concrete slab provides a flat, solid substrate. To the right of the grill, a stainless-steel sink helps out during meal preparation and cleanup. Below the sink, a metal door opens to below-counter storage and access to plumbing. Though this barbecue wraps around a column that supports one end of a patio trellis, you can straighten the back wall to simplify the design and make it suitable for any location.

Building Notes

Buy the grill, sink, and metal access door before starting construction so you can verify measurements as you build. Because of the counter's curved edge, many tiles must be cut. For this work, it pays to rent the type of "wet" tile-cutting saw that shoots water on the diamond blade as it cuts.

1 Start by creating forms for a 6-inch-thick concrete slab the shape of the barbecue's footprint. To do this, excavate about 5 inches deep, then form the straight backside of the slab by nailing a 1 by 4 to stakes driven into the ground. To form the curve, fasten a length of redwood bender-

board to the right end of the back wall and secure it in place with a stake. Bend it to form the curve of the front wall and drive stakes into the ground to hold it. Level the tops of the forms at the height of the slab and nail them to the stakes.

2 Strengthen the slab with a grid of $1/2$-inch steel reinforcing bar placed every 12 inches and held off the ground about 3 inches with small pieces of broken blocks or brick.

3 Run a gas pipe and electrical conduit through the slab (see pages 131 and 136–137), stub them up above the slab's level, and wrap the top ends with duct tape to protect them from mortar. The gas pipe should rise up through the slab where its shutoff valve can be accessed through the metal door. The electrical conduit should stub up where it will pass through the cells of the concrete blocks and rise vertically to the receptacle locations (run the vertical sections of conduit up about 4 feet after the slab has been poured). Cast the concrete slab as discussed on page 110 and allow it to cure.

4 Begin building the concrete-block walls, starting with the straight back wall, using the techniques discussed on page 120. Continue with the curved front wall, following the slab's curve. Check from block to block with a level as you work. Leave an opening for the access door and a recess for the barbecue grill, sized according to the manufacturer's specifications. Support the concrete blocks that span the doorway with angle iron as discussed on page 118. You can mortar the door's frame

MATERIALS CHECKLIST

Gas grill

Prehung metal access door

Stainless-steel sink, faucet, & plumbing

Gas pipe, shutoff valve, & connections

Electrical conduit, cable, boxes, & GFCI receptacles

Ready-mix concrete (or concrete ingredients)

$1/2$" & $3/8$" steel reinforcing bar

Lumber & plywood or scrap for concrete forms

$1/4$" hardboard for concrete forms

Benderboard & stakes

2"-diameter PVC pipe (scrap piece)

Concrete blocks

Mortar mix for concrete block

3"x3" angle iron

Various masonry screws & concrete nails

Countertop tile

Tile spacers

Stain-resistant grout for tile

Grout sealer

Sand stucco mix

into place as you build or add it later, fastening it with concrete screws. Scrape the joints as you work, but don't bother striking them because they will be hidden by the stucco.

5 Place a 5-foot-long $^1/_2$-inch steel reinforcing bar vertically in every other cell and a $^3/_8$-inch reinforcing bar horizontally along each course of blocks (you'll have to bend the horizontal bars into an arc for the curved wall). Once you've installed four courses of blocks and the reinforcing bar, fill all of the cores with grout (see page 104). Do not grout the cells where the conduit is located.

6 Next build the forms for casting the countertop's concrete slab. Make a temporary platform inside the unit from several pieces of scrap $^5/_8$-inch plywood so it can be taken apart and pulled out from inside after the concrete sets up. Support it on temporary 1-by-4 ledgers fastened to the concrete blocks with concrete nails. Prop the platform from underneath with 2 by 4s for additional support.

7 To contain the concrete slab along the curved section and create a slight overhang, tack a piece of redwood benderboard to the blocks flush with the top blocks. Then rip lengths of $^1/_4$-inch hardboard, 6 inches wide, and fasten them to the benderboard with concrete nails so they extend 3 inches above the blocks (see the bottom illustration on the facing page). Nail short pieces of the hardboard flush to the blocks in the barbecue area. Also use hardboard to create a fence that

will keep concrete out of the sink's location, sizing this according to the sink's cutout specifications.

8 When the forms are complete, bend the vertical reinforcing bars and wire them to additional lengths of $^1/_2$-inch reinforcing bar to create a 12-inch grid within the countertop slab area. Support this grid about 1 inch above the platform with small pieces of broken concrete blocks. Pour the 3-inch slab as discussed on page 110, then strike and trowel it until it's level and smooth. Before pouring the small section where the barbecue rests, put a 4-inch length of 2-inch PVC pipe upright on the platform. Then, after the slab has set up, you can remove the wood support and pull out the PVC pipe, leaving a hole through which you can feed the gas line. Allow the concrete to cure for several days.

9 Use a hand grinder with a masonry-cutting blade (or use a brickset) to make holes in the concrete blocks for the electrical boxes. Cut off the conduit, mount the boxes, and complete the wiring (see page 136).

10 Apply the countertop tile using the methods discussed on page 124. Work forward from the straight back wall. Wait for the mortar to cure (one to two days), then apply grout (see page 128).

11 Apply stucco to the outside of the concrete block as discussed on page 119. After the stucco has cured, install the barbecue unit following the manufacturer's directions. Also install the sink and faucet, as discussed on page 132.

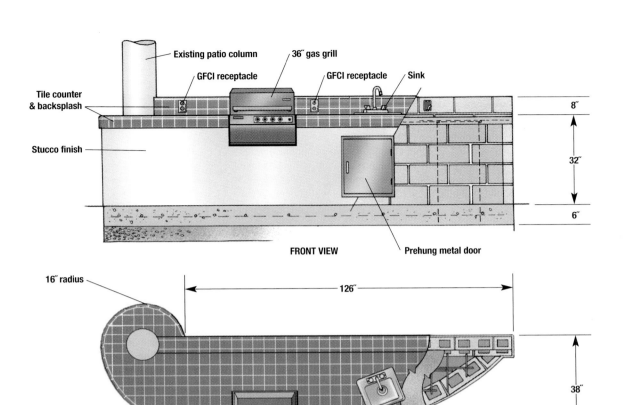

Existing patio column

GFCI receptacle

36″ gas grill

GFCI receptacle

Sink

Tile counter & backsplash

Stucco finish

8″

32″

6″

FRONT VIEW

Prehung metal door

16″ radius

126″

38″

TOP VIEW

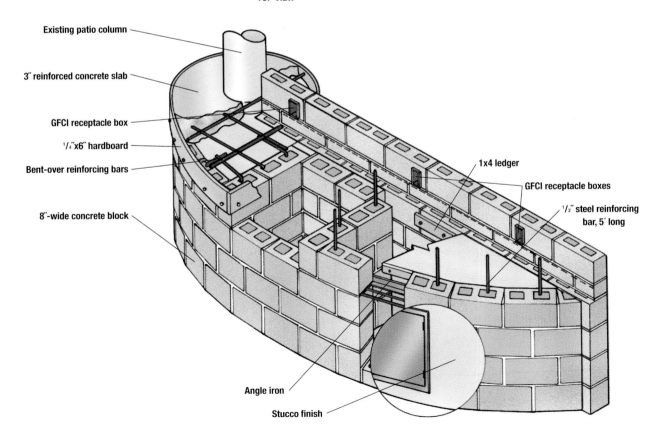

Existing patio column

3″ reinforced concrete slab

GFCI receptacle box

1/4″x6″ hardboard

Bent-over reinforcing bars

8″-wide concrete block

1x4 ledger

GFCI receptacle boxes

1/2″ steel reinforcing bar, 5′ long

Angle iron

Stucco finish

WALL-ATTACHED COOKING COUNTER

This stylish barbecue, featured on the cover, is a delightful center of attraction for a contemporary outdoor entertaining area.
Landscape architects: Ransohoff, Blanchfield & Jones, Inc.
Mason: Lehmann Landscaping Co.

Like an indoor kitchen that has moved outdoors, this cooking center features a counter that runs adjacent to the home's wall and houses a gas grill, sink, and storage cabinets. The top is surfaced with durable glazed ceramic tile and the base is stucco-coated to match the house's exterior.

Design Details

The barbecue cabinet is built of concrete blocks that have been given a finish coat of stucco. Underneath the countertop tile, $1^1/_8$-inch marine-grade plywood provides a base. Note: Because plywood is a combustible material, pay special attention to the grill manufacturer's specifications for proper clearances. For other countertop constructions, see page 124.

A stainless-steel sink to the left of the grill makes meal preparation and cleanup easy; stainless-steel cabinet doors at the base of the unit lead to storage as well as gas and water shutoffs. Although this barbecue angles to align with the house wall, it is an easy job to modify the plans for a straight wall—in fact, this unit could be built free-standing elsewhere in the yard.

Building Notes

Buy the grill, sink, and metal cabinet doors before you begin construction and have them on-site as you build; size the base unit's dimensions to fit them according to the manufacturers' clearance specifications. Because the unit is adjacent to the house's walls, plumbing, gas, and electrical connections can be routed through the walls to the unit. Still, unless you have experience in these areas, have a professional plumber and electrician do the rough-ins.

1 Start by trenching for the barbecue's footing. The one shown stands on a perimeter footing that is 12 inches wide and 18 inches deep (12 inches below the frost line). Also excavate for a 4-inch-thick concrete slab that is the shape of the barbecue.

2 Run $1/_2$-inch reinforcing bars horizontally in the footings, and strengthen the slab with reinforcing bars placed every 12 inches and held off the ground about 2 inches with fragments of broken blocks or brick. Cut the reinforcing bars with a steel-cutting blade mounted on a power circular saw. Be sure to wear safety glasses and gloves.

3 Have a plumber run gas and water lines and the sink drain through the wall and stub them out according to the locations specified in your final plans. Be sure you'll be able to reach the shutoff valves for the gas and water supplies through the cabinet doorway. Make sure that the electrical conduit stubs out at the receptacle locations.

4 Cast the concrete slab as discussed on page 110 and allow two to three days for it to cure.

5 Build the concrete-block walls starting with the 8-inch-wide back course, using the techniques discussed on page 120. Continue with the sides and finish with the 6-inch-wide front wall course. Be sure to keep the courses straight and level (check them frequently as you work). Leave openings for the stainless-steel doors and a

MATERIALS CHECKLIST
Gas grill
Prehung stainless-steel doors
Stainless-steel sink, faucet, & plumbing
Gas pipe, shutoff valve, & connections
Electrical conduit, cable, boxes, & GFCI receptacles
Ready-mix concrete (or concrete ingredients)
$1/_2$" steel reinforcing bar
Concrete blocks
Mortar mix for concrete block
3"x3" angle iron
Marine-grade plywood ($1^1/_8$")
Masonry anchors & lag bolts
Various masonry screws & concrete nails
Countertop tile
Tile spacers
Stain-resistant grout for tile
Grout sealer
Sand stucco mix

recess for the barbecue grill, sized according to the manufacturer's specifications. Support the concrete blocks across the top of the doorways with angle iron, as discussed on page 118, and run $1/2$-inch steel reinforcing bar centered horizontally every other course. Scrape excess mortar from the joints as you work but don't bother to strike them because the block will receive a stucco finish.

6   Place $1/2$-inch steel reinforcing bar vertically in every other concrete-block cell. Then fill all of the cores with grout. Do not grout the cells where electrical conduit is located.

7   Next, fasten angle iron horizontally along the block walls to support the plywood countertop base (see the top illustration on the facing page). Drill through the angle iron with a metal-drilling bit every 12 inches and fasten with lag screws inserted into masonry anchors, as discussed on page 118.

8   Cut the $1^{1}/8$-inch marine-plywood base to size using a power circular saw. Coat both

surfaces and all edges with paint or high-quality water repellent to prevent damage from moisture. Fasten the plywood in place by screwing into its underside through the holes in the angle iron.

9   Use a hand grinder with a masonry-cutting blade (or use a brickset) to make holes in the concrete blocks for the electrical boxes. Cut off the conduit and mount the boxes.

10 Apply the countertop tile following the methods discussed on page 127. Wait for the mortar to cure (one to two days), then apply grout (see page 128).

11 Follow the manufacturer's instructions to install the stainless-steel access doors.

12 Stucco the outside of the concrete block as discussed on page 119. After the stucco has cured, install the barbecue unit, following the manufacturer's directions. Install the stainless-steel sink and the faucet as discussed on page 132. Finally, complete the electrical wiring for the GFCI receptacles (see page 136).

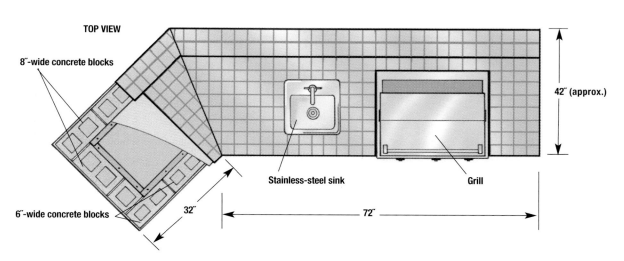

TOP VIEW

8″-wide concrete blocks

6″-wide concrete blocks

Stainless-steel sink

Grill

42″ (approx.)

32″

72″

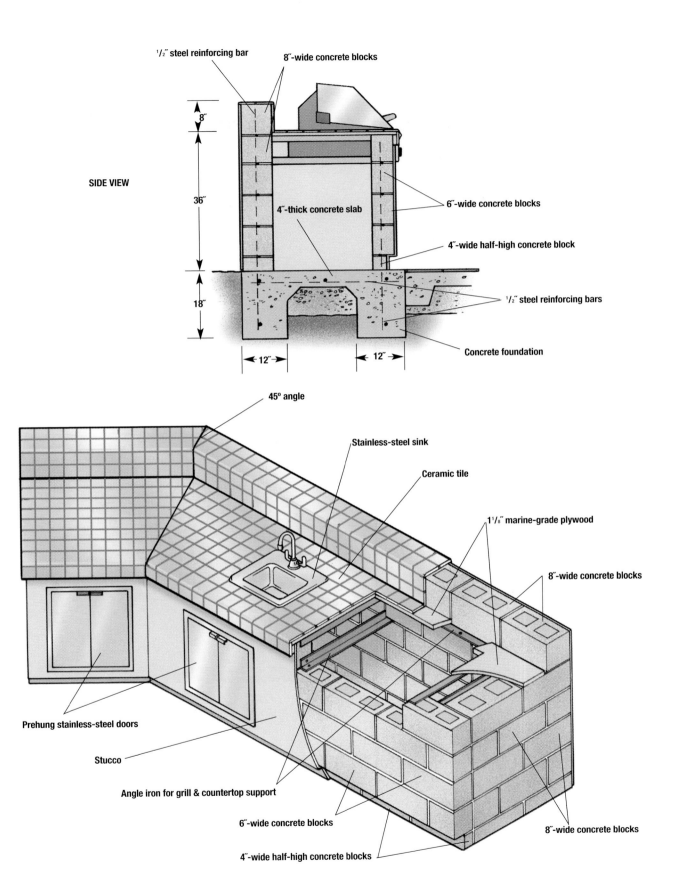

½" steel reinforcing bar

8"-wide concrete blocks

SIDE VIEW

8"

36"

18"

4"-thick concrete slab

6"-wide concrete blocks

4"-wide half-high concrete block

½" steel reinforcing bars

Concrete foundation

12"

12"

45° angle

Stainless-steel sink

Ceramic tile

1⅛" marine-grade plywood

8"-wide concrete blocks

Prehung stainless-steel doors

Stucco

Angle iron for grill & countertop support

6"-wide concrete blocks

4"-wide half-high concrete blocks

8"-wide concrete blocks

BLUESTONE BARBECUE

The natural beauty and rugged texture of quarried stone
are featured in this distinctive backyard cooking center
built on an elegant bluestone patio.
Landscape architect: Michael B. Yandle
Masonry contractor: KG Masonry
Landscape contractor: Bertotti Landscaping Inc.

Though the structure of this cooking center looks like it's made of solid stone, it's actually concrete block veneered with 5-to-6-inch-thick pieces of charcoal-gray wall rock, grouted with black mortar. The exceptions to this construction are the curved backsplash behind the grill and a wall at the left side of the unit, both of which are built entirely of stone.

Design Details

To match the patio, this cooking center features a generous Connecticut bluestone counter. It is equipped with a drop-in 41-inch-wide stainless-steel gas grill, a single-bowl sink with a tall gooseneck faucet, and two GFCI-protected electrical outlets. The grill is flanked by two under-counter storage cabinets with 24-by-30-inch doors, built by a local cabinetmaker. Recessed slightly from the stone face, the doors are protected not only from the elements but from any spills that might drip off the counter.

Building Notes

The professional-quality rotisserie grill is hooked up to a natural gas line, eliminating the inconvenience of having to refill propane tanks. The appliances were purchased first, then the $2\frac{1}{2}$-inch-thick counter was cut precisely by the stoneyard's mason to accept the drop-in grill and the sink.

1. Cast the concrete foundation and slab (for more about casting this type of foundation, see page 110). Before pouring concrete, be sure to have the sink plumbing, gas line, and electrical conduit roughed-in (see pages 131–137). Allow the footing to cure for three to five days before beginning construction with the concrete block and stone.

2. Start construction of the walls by laying the first course of 6-inch-wide blocks that forms the back wall of the barbecue. For information on building with concrete block and stone, see pages 120 and 122.

3. From these blocks, work forward, laying courses of 8-inch-wide blocks for the side walls, 6-inch-wide blocks for the perpendicular center walls, and 4-inch-wide blocks for the front wall. Continue laying courses, using the techniques discussed on page 120. Note in the illustrations on page 89 that you will need to make filler pieces by cutting parts from full-sized blocks.

4. As you build every other course, lay a #4 ($\frac{1}{2}$-inch-diameter) steel reinforcing bar horizontally across the center of the blocks to tie them together. Also insert a reinforcing bar vertically in every other block core and fill the cores with grout. You must mix very thin grout without gravel (use masonry sand) for the 4-inch-wide blocks so the grout can be poured into the narrow hollows.

5. Use half-high (4-inch-high) blocks to span across the top of the storage cabinet doorways; support these blocks with angle iron.

6. When the block walls are completed, use a trowel to spread mortar onto the outer surfaces of about 4 square feet of the block. Spread more mortar onto the back

MATERIALS CHECKLIST

Gas grill

Prehung stainless-steel door(s)

Stainless-steel sink, faucet & plumbing

Gas pipe, shutoff valve, & connections

Electrical conduit, cable, boxes, & GFCI receptacles

2 custom wood 24˝x30˝ doors & hardware

Custom bluestone counter & backsplash

5˝ to 6˝ charcoal gray wall rock & solid stone

Ready-mix concrete (or concrete ingredients)

Lumber & plywood or scrap for concrete forms

³/₄˝ plywood (for a template)

¹/₂˝ steel reinforcing bar

Concrete blocks

Mortar mix for concrete block

3˝x3˝ angle iron

Lime-free mortar mix for stone

Black masonry dye

1x6 redwood

of each stone and press it to the mortared blocks, starting at the bottom of the walls and working your way up. If you're using irregularly shaped stones like the ones shown in this project, try to choose pieces that fit closely together. Continue this process, working in approximately 4-foot-square areas.

7   Before building the back wall's eyebrow-shaped curve, note that the countertop rests on the block walls and a 1-by-8-inch bluestone backsplash sits on top of the counter and is recessed into the stone. Be sure to allow for both the countertop and the backsplash as you build the back wall from stone. Cut a template for the curve from a sheet of ³/₄-inch plywood, using a saber saw. As you build, hold up this template periodically to check for uniformity. As you near the top of the template, use increasingly smaller stones to finish the curved shape.

8   Once all the stones are laid, mix up some mortar in a wheelbarrow, sprinkle in black masonry dye, and mix again. Apply the mortar to the joints between the stones with a grout bag or a trowel and smooth out the mortar joints with a convex jointer or a dowel.

9   Once you've built the base and your sink and appliances are on the site, measure for the countertop and order it to size (or—better yet—have the stone mason come out and take the measurements). Be sure to give the cutout pattern for the sink to the stoneyard so that the sink hole can be precut. Have the bluestone deliv-

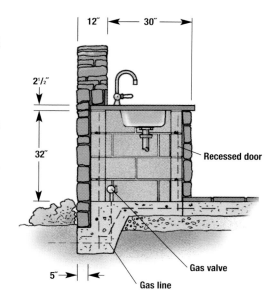

ered on the day you intend to install it, and make sure to invite a few friends over—you will need help lifting this very heavy piece in place.

10 Spread a thick bed of mortar along the tops of the stone-veneered walls, then install the countertop, allowing it to overhang the front wall by 2 inches. Then install the bluestone backsplash along the rear of the counter.

11 To construct the wall to the left of the grill, lay stones as you did for the back wall, working from bottom to top. Choose the flattest stones you can find for the top course.

12 You can make the cabinet doors yourself from a weather- and decay-resistant wood, such as cedar or redwood. Install a 1-by-6 redwood frame in the block doorways, fastening the wood to the block with concrete nails. Then hinge the doors to the frame. Finally, install the sink, grill, and electrical receptacles.

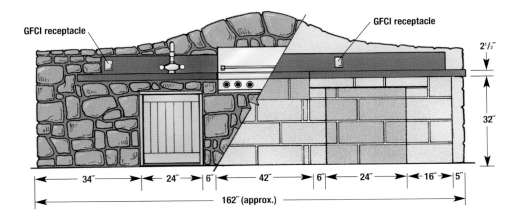

GFCI receptacle

GFCI receptacle

2¹/₂″

32″

34″ 24″ 6″ 42″ 6″ 24″ 16″ 5″

162″ (approx.)

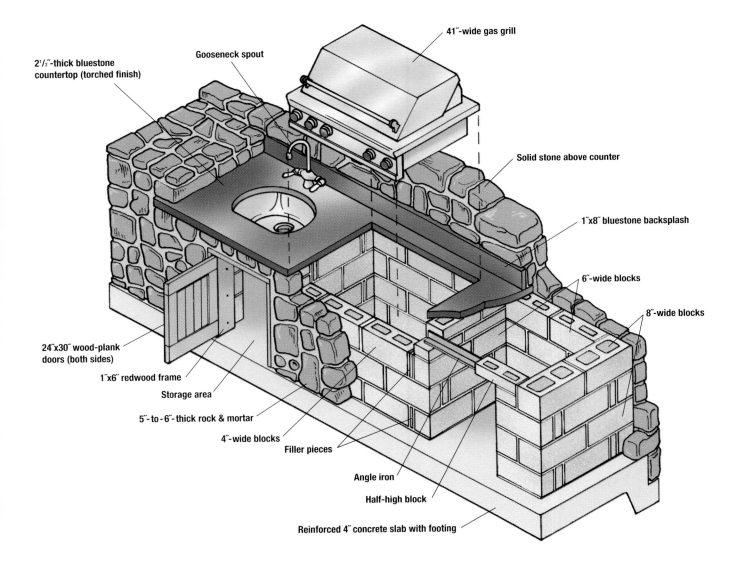

41″-wide gas grill

Gooseneck spout

2¹/₂″-thick bluestone
countertop (torched finish)

Solid stone above counter

1″x8″ bluestone backsplash

6″-wide blocks

8″-wide blocks

24″x30″ wood-plank
doors (both sides)

1″x6″ redwood frame

Storage area

5″-to-6″-thick rock & mortar

4″-wide blocks

Filler pieces

Angle iron

Half-high block

Reinforced 4″ concrete slab with footing

ITALIAN PIZZA OVEN

A pizza oven allows the cook to prepare an incomparable array of foods with a uniquely smoky flavor.
Landscape architects: Jack Chandler & Associates

An Italian pizza oven may be the ultimate in outdoor cooking. It not only produces pizza with a bubbly top and light, crispy crust, it also bakes breads and roasts meats with a slightly smoky taste.

Design Details

The oven itself, barely visible from the exterior, is available only as an import from Italy. It is made of *cotto refrattario*, a special refractory terra-cotta clay with a precise amount of alumina content. The material is porous, so it can absorb steam and produce breads with crisp crusts. The oven has its own floor, to ensure that the food being cooked is completely surrounded by porous materials. The upper surround is always curved, to allow the heat to circulate freely. The flue is positioned just behind the door to remove smoke efficiently and allow the food to be seen easily.

The oven surround must have a massively thick floor; other than this, it can be constructed in any number of designs. The surround shown in this project has a metal hip roof, but a gable or flat roof would perform just as well. Any sort of facing—brick, tile, rubble, or the ashlar shown—will work just fine.

In the usual outdoor arrangement (these ovens can be installed indoors as well if properly vented), the oven is placed at a comfortable height—about 48 inches off the ground—and the space below is used to store firewood.

Building Notes

A pizza oven is a serious barbecue, requiring a significant budget—the oven alone runs several thousand dollars—as well as skilled labor. The oven must rest on a 15-inch-thick reinforced concrete-and-sand slab, which must be formed in the air rather than on the ground. Unless

The refractory component of a pizza oven can be fitted into any of many types of structures. This rubble-stone oven offers a rustic, natural look.

you're experienced at masonry work, you're probably better off leaving the actual construction in the hands of a masonry contractor. Before you start building, purchase the oven.

The directions on these pages concentrate on the underlying structure. Face the concrete block and cover the roof with the materials of your choice.

Three concrete pours—one for the slab on the ground, and two for the slab under the oven—make this a time-consuming project. Allow at least two days between each of the pours for the concrete to cure.

1 Pour the foundation. In addition to the 15-inch-thick slab for the oven, the entire structure must rest on a solid slab of reinforced concrete, with footings at least 24 inches deep, to support the walls (see page 110 for information on casting a slab).

2 Once the slab on the ground has cured, snap chalk lines for the perimeter of the

MATERIALS CHECKLIST

Italian pizza oven, complete with flue, door, & insulating blanket

Gravel

Sand

Lumber & plywood or scrap for concrete forms

Building paper

Ready-mix concrete (or concrete ingredients)

$1/2''$ & $3/8''$ steel reinforcing bar

8'' anchor bolts

Concrete blocks

Mortar mix for concrete block

Lime-free mortar mix for stone

Refractory mortar

Vermiculite

Materials for facing & roofing

Zero-clearance chimney pipe

structure. The unit shown here is a three-sided structure, but you may choose to build partial walls on the fourth side. Mix mortar and lay four courses of 8-inch concrete block. Be sure to strengthen the block with reinforcing bar (see page 120 for detailed information on building with concrete block).

3   Build strong forms to hold a 6-inch concrete pour. Cut nine 4-by-4 posts to $2^{1}/_{4}$ inches shorter than the top of the block wall; three 2 by 4s to the inside length of the walls; and two pieces of $^{3}/_{4}$-inch plywood to fit snugly inside the walls. Screw the 2 by 4s, laid flat, to the underside of plywood pieces, one running along the middle and the other two about 4 inches from the outside edges. Raise the plywood-and-2-by-4 piece into position, and support it with the 4-by-4 posts. The top of the plywood should be flush with the top of the concrete blocks; cut or shim the posts if you need to make any adjustments.

4   Cut four 2 by 8s and screw them together to form a frame that fits snugly around the block walls. Position them so their tops are 6 inches above the plywood, and support them with eight 2 by 4s to keep them from slipping down. Attach four 2-by-6 angle braces to the 2 by 8s to keep them from bellying out when you pour the concrete. Cut and lay a gridwork of $^{1}/_{2}$-inch reinforcing bar and pour the concrete.

5   After the concrete has cured for several days, remove the forms. Lay a single course of 6-inch concrete block on top of the perimeter of the concrete. Let the mortar

cure for at least a day, then fill the cavity with 6 inches of dry sand.

6   Next, build forms for the top layer of concrete, which will be 3 inches thick. Place 2 by 6s around the perimeter so they extend 3 inches above the sand and support them with 2 by 4s to keep them from slipping down. If your oven requires a shelf in front, support it with $^{3}/_{4}$-inch plywood and 4-by-4 posts. Lay a sheet of building paper on top of the sand. Cut and lay reinforcing bar, and pour the slab. Then trowel the surface level and smooth.

7   Once the concrete has cured, install the oven according to the manufacturer's directions. Lay the floor pieces in a dry run on the concrete to establish correct positioning and check for level. Trowel a thin layer of refractory mortar on the concrete, and set the floor pieces in. Recheck for level. Assemble the four crown pieces, then mortar in the arch. Attach the flue pieces by drilling holes and driving masonry screws. Cover the oven with a thermal blanket supplied by the oven maker. Install the door in the same way. Finish the block walls and grout in 8-inch anchor bolts at the corners.

8   Attach chimney pipe sections according to your plans and local codes ("zero-clearance" pipe is often the best choice). Fill the cavity around the oven with vermiculite. Then finish the exterior of the walls by facing them with stone or brick (see pages 114 and 122). To make an oven like this one, have a sheet-metal or roofing contractor fabricate a copper roof to fit and attach it to the anchor bolts.

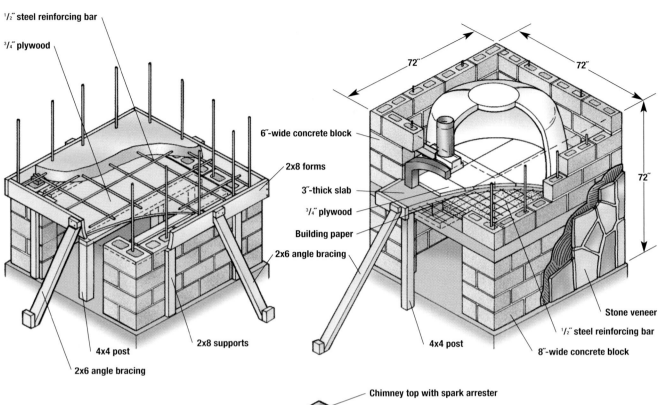

½″ steel reinforcing bar

¾″ plywood

6″-wide concrete block

2x8 forms

3″-thick slab

¾″ plywood

Building paper

2x6 angle bracing

2x8 supports

4x4 post

2x6 angle bracing

72″

72″

72″

Stone veneer

½″ steel reinforcing bar

8″-wide concrete block

4x4 post

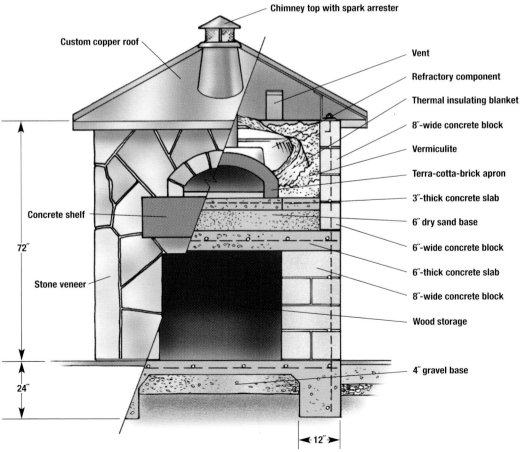

Chimney top with spark arrester

Custom copper roof

Vent

Refractory component

Thermal insulating blanket

8″-wide concrete block

Vermiculite

Terra-cotta-brick apron

3″-thick concrete slab

6″ dry sand base

6″-wide concrete block

6″-thick concrete slab

8″-wide concrete block

Wood storage

4″ gravel base

Concrete shelf

72″

Stone veneer

24″

12″

Materials & Techniques

Some of the projects in this book may look a bit intimidating, particularly if you haven't had much experience with do-it-yourself projects. Though it's true that some involve a range of tasks—from masonry to electrical work—when taken one at a time, most are actually quite manageable. With a few basic skills and tools, you may be amazed at what you can accomplish.

Clearly, a simple brick barbecue is far easier to build than an extensive outdoor kitchen replete with appliances, utilities, and other amenities. Though building an outdoor kitchen isn't quite as involved as building an indoor one, it does take significant planning and preparation. Before beginning to build, be sure to refer to the planning chapter, Cooking Outdoors, beginning on page 4.

This chapter touches on all aspects of building an outdoor cooking center, from buying materials and acquiring the needed tools and gear to building the unit. You'll find information on preparing the site, working with barbecue-building materials, and installing amenities such as water, gas, and electrical lines to the unit.

As with any building project, check first with your building department about local codes.

BARBECUE-BUILDING TOOLS

Building a barbecue may include tasks that range from pouring a concrete foundation to building masonry walls to installing plumbing and electrical lines. The tools needed for these jobs vary widely, from digging and yard-preparation tools to masonry and carpentry tools. You might also need a cement mixer if you'll be pouring concrete or mixing a lot of mortar. Keep in mind that almost any tool can be rented.

SAFETY GEAR

When working with many of the tools on these pages, you'll need basic safety equipment, too, such as gloves and safety glasses.

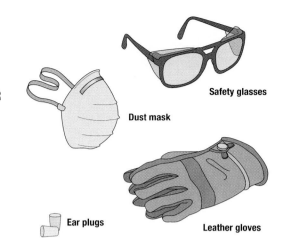

Safety glasses

Dust mask

Ear plugs

Leather gloves

YARD PREPARATION TOOLS

You'll need a shovel and/or spade for digging and a steel rake for grading an area where concrete will be poured. A wheelbarrow is also a must for moving soil and can be used for mixing and pouring concrete.

Spade

Steel rake

Wheelbarrow

Square shovel

ELECTRICAL TOOLS

Lineman's pliers combine serrated jaws designed to twist wires with cutters to snip wire. Long-nose pliers cut wire and are particularly handy for forming hooks at stripped wire ends. Diagonal-cutting pliers cut wire. Wire strippers remove insulation from wires of various gauges. A neon tester determines whether or not a circuit is "hot" (turned on).

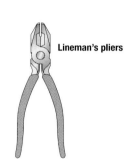

Lineman's pliers

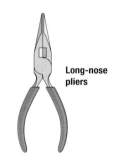

Long-nose pliers

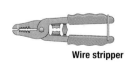

Wire stripper

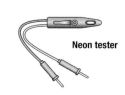

Neon tester

Diagonal-cutting pliers

CARPENTRY TOOLS

For building the framing, hanging cabinet doors, and various other barbecue-building tasks, you'll need an assortment of basic carpentry tools.

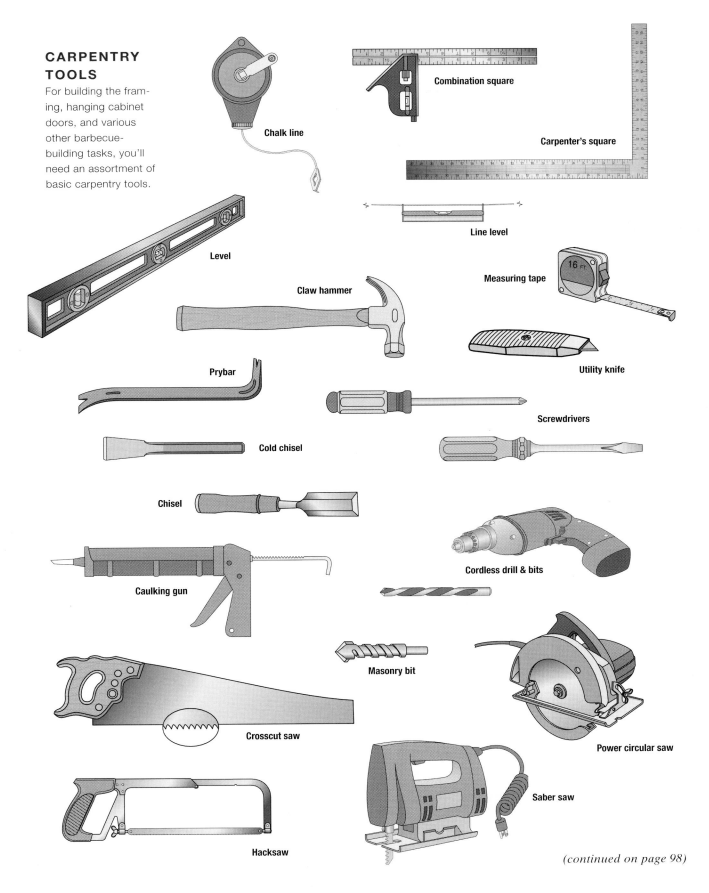

Chalk line

Combination square

Carpenter's square

Line level

Measuring tape

Level

Claw hammer

Utility knife

Prybar

Screwdrivers

Cold chisel

Chisel

Cordless drill & bits

Caulking gun

Masonry bit

Crosscut saw

Power circular saw

Saber saw

Hacksaw

(continued on page 98)

(continued from page 97)

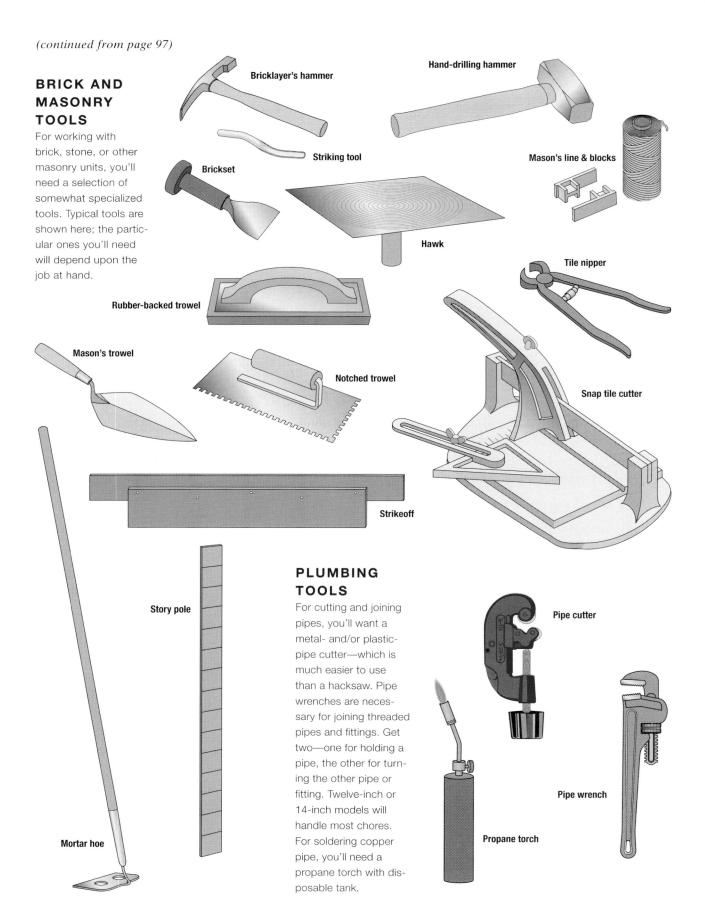

BRICK AND MASONRY TOOLS

For working with brick, stone, or other masonry units, you'll need a selection of somewhat specialized tools. Typical tools are shown here; the particular ones you'll need will depend upon the job at hand.

Bricklayer's hammer

Hand-drilling hammer

Striking tool

Brickset

Mason's line & blocks

Hawk

Tile nipper

Rubber-backed trowel

Mason's trowel

Notched trowel

Snap tile cutter

Strikeoff

Story pole

Mortar hoe

PLUMBING TOOLS

For cutting and joining pipes, you'll want a metal- and/or plastic-pipe cutter—which is much easier to use than a hacksaw. Pipe wrenches are necessary for joining threaded pipes and fittings. Get two—one for holding a pipe, the other for turning the other pipe or fitting. Twelve-inch or 14-inch models will handle most chores. For soldering copper pipe, you'll need a propane torch with disposable tank.

Pipe cutter

Propane torch

Pipe wrench

CHOOSING & BUYING MATERIALS

For both appearance and durability, most outdoor cooking centers are made primarily of concrete block, brick, stone, or other masonry materials, as well as plywood, lumber, and related construction materials. In this section, we'll take a closer look at barbecue-building materials to help with your decision making and purchasing, then we'll move on to discuss techniques for working with these materials.

Brick

Brick is one of the most frequently used barbecue-building materials. Uniform in shape, it provides a handsome surface that complements nearly every architectural style and looks at ease in almost every outdoor setting. Brick is available in a range of colors, sizes, and finishes and can be laid in a number of patterns, from basic to complex.

Bricks are made of various clay and shale mixtures, which are carefully dried, then fired in a kiln at very high temperatures to set permanently. Two basic types are commonly used for building: common brick, which has a rough texture, and the more expensive face brick, which is slick. Most people prefer the casual, irregular look of common brick, but it is also porous, making it more likely to stain and be damaged by absorbed moisture.

Firebrick, slightly larger and heavier than common brick, is made of clay that can withstand the severe heat that will cause common brick to break up. Firebrick is customarily used to line fireboxes of traditional wood- or charcoal-burning barbecues. It is sensitive to moisture and cold, though, and will disintegrate if directly exposed to severe winter weather. In areas where heavy frosts are prevalent, "hard-burned" common brick is often used to line fireboxes.

Used brick has uneven surfaces and streaks of old mortar that give it an aged, informal look. Taken from old construction, true used brick is in short supply. As a result, many manufacturers produce new bricks that look used by chipping them and splashing them with mortar and paint. Manufactured "used" brick costs about the same as the genuine article and is more consistent in quality.

Most brick is made in modular sizes—that is, the length is a simple multiple of the width, which simplifies ordering and fitting. The standard modular brick measures 8 inches long by 4 inches wide by $2\frac{1}{2}$ inches high. A "split" brick is the same length and width but only about 1 inch thick. This is a

TYPES OF BRICK

Common brick

Face brick

Firebrick

Used brick

New brick made to look used

popular and cost-effective choice for brick-veneer barbecue construction.

Many other sizes are available, at larger brickyards, in sizes ranging from 12 by 4 inches to 16 by 12 inches and in various thicknesses. Note that all of these dimensions include the width of a standard $^1/_2$-inch mortar joint, so the actual dimensions of the brick are less by that measurement.

All outdoor bricks are graded according to their ability to withstand weathering. If you live where freezing temperatures may occur, buy only those graded SX. Other grades recognized by the Brick Institute of America are MX, for applications where freezing temperatures do not occur, and NX, for interior applications.

Concrete Block

For fast, inexpensive masonry-barbecue construction, it is hard to beat concrete block (also called "concrete masonry units," or "CMUs"). These rugged, non-combustible units make decorative and structurally sound barbecues. Working with them is also

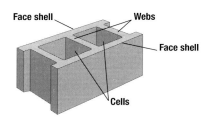

Face shell · Webs · Face shell · Cells

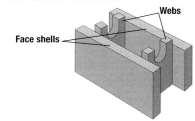

Webs · Face shells

well within the capacity of most do-it-yourselfers. A barbecue that appears to be made of brick, stone, or stucco is often built primarily of concrete block—and then given one of these veneers.

Blocks are produced in a wide variety of colors and shapes, and in several modular sizes. As with bricks, dimensions are nominal, including a standard $^3/_8$-inch mortar joint. In addition to the 16-by-8-by-8-inch standard size, blocks come in 4-, 6-, 10- and 12-inch widths and 4-inch ("half") heights.

You can also buy architectural blocks that resemble hand-hewn stone or polished granite. Among these are "split-face" blocks, which have a coarse, irregular texture; these are available in several earth tones.

Conventional blocks have two equal-size holes (or "cells") that run side by side through their centers, from top to bottom. As the blocks are stacked, these holes line up; typically, reinforcing steel rods are placed inside some of the cavities, then all the holes are filled with grout. This provides the wall with virtually monolithic strength.

Another variety of concrete block is designed for building in the same interlocking pattern, but without the need for mortar

TYPES OF CONCRETE BLOCK

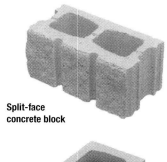

Split-face concrete block

Standard concrete block stretcher

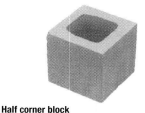

Half corner block

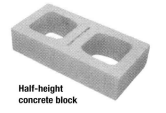

Half-height concrete block

joints. A mortarless block wall, well-reinforced and grouted, is as strong as one built with mortared blocks. In one popular system, the block units are available in 6- or 8-inch-wide stretchers, corners, and half corners. Widely accepted by building codes, mortarless blocks are available in most home centers with leaflets describing how to lay them.

In some regions, you can even buy "autoclaved" solid blocks that are laid-up with a very strong thin-set mortar. Filled with thousands of tiny air pockets, these lightweight blocks can be cut like wood and you can drive a nail or screw into them. A standard 8-by-8-by-24-inch block weighs only about 28 pounds, as opposed to cast concrete, which weighs in at 150 pounds per cubic foot.

Another great advantage of autoclaved blocks is that they are suitable for high-heat applications—an 8-inch-thick block has an 8-hour fire rating—so they can be used very near wooden structures. Currently, this material is available only in the Southeast, Mexico, and Japan; the cost of shipping to other regions is prohibitive.

When planning your barbecue, first pick the concrete units you'll be using, then adjust the overall dimensions of the barbecue and its footing to suit the unit's size. By using fractional sizes of blocks, you may never have to cut a block.

Stone

When rugged good looks are important, stone is a premium choice. Stoneyards supply uncut (rubble) or cut (ashlar) stone of various types. Ashlar stone is more expensive but far easier to work with because it has a more squared-off shape. Both types are laid up with mortar.

The availability and cost of different types, shapes, sizes, and colors of stone depend on the region in which you live. Visit a stone or masonry supply in your area to see what's available.

Marble and granite are the toughest and longest-wearing of the options. Earth-toned sandstone, limestone, and other sedimentary stones have a chalky or gritty texture and are more porous. Dense, smooth slate is a

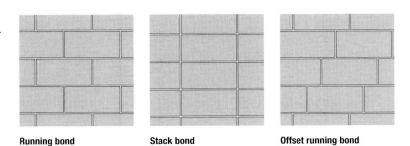

Running bond   Stack bond   Offset running bond

BOND PATTERNS

Basic bond patterns for brick and concrete block are shown here. Running bond is the strongest and most common. Stack bond requires extreme care when aligning vertical joints to avoid an irregular look, but if well reinforced, also works. Offset running bond has a more irregular, random appearance, but when using concrete blocks this method does not allow cores to line up for easy steel and grout reinforcement.

fine-grained metamorphic rock.

Flagstone is any flat stone that is either naturally thin or split from rock that cleaves easily. It is usually a subdued color—buff, yellow, brownish red, or gray—and irregularly shaped. Flagstone generally ranges in thickness from $1/2$ inch to 2 inches. It is much more expensive than brick, which is more costly than concrete. Also, some types of flagstone soil easily and are difficult to clean.

Buy your stone from a reputable dealer and ask how it was mined. Stone that was blasted out of the ground may contain tiny fissures that will encourage deterioration of the wall. For locations where appearance is key, such as a countertop, hand-pick the pieces.

If you figure the cubic volume of your barbecue's walls, your dealer can calculate the quantity of stone you'll need. Some dealers price by the cubic yard; others sell by the ton. To calculate the volume of each wall, multiply its height by its width by its length in yards. Stone usually weighs around 125 pounds per cubic foot or 3,375 pounds per cubic yard.

Rubble stone will have a greater volume per ton than trimmed stone because of the voids between the rocks. When it is loaded in a truck, rubble stone might run as much as three parts rock to one part void—25 percent air. Once you begin fitting the stones into a wall, you'll find their volume considerably reduced. Try to inspect before you buy. Stones should harmonize in color and texture, and whichever type you choose should have a good range of sizes. For best effect, the face area of the largest stones should be about six times the face area of the smallest.

Alternatives to Stone

Building with stone (see page 122) is a bit tricky because of stone's heavy weight and irregular shapes. Most masons prefer to

TYPES OF STONE

Rubble stone

Rough-cut flagstone

Imitation stone

Ashlar stone

Roughly squared cobblestone

Slate

Tumbled marble tile

Square adobe block

Adobe paver

achieve a similar look by building a barbecue's structure with concrete block, then cladding the block with a stone veneer, stone tiles, or synthetic stone.

Many stone types are available precut to rectangular shapes in the form of tiles or stone veneer. You can also find hand-cut stones in random-size squares and rectangles. As a rule, stone tiles—such as granite—and stone veneers are far less expensive than ashlar stone.

Synthetic stone veneers, made of cement mixtures, often look surprisingly like the real thing. You may want to consider using them for their significant cost- and labor-saving qualities.

Synthetic stone tiles mimic the look of granite and sandstone but offer the advantages of glazed tiles. Colors include black and various shades of gray and beige, in patterns of varying intensity.

Adobe

The Southwest's version of the mud brick, adobe is one of the world's oldest building materials. Found almost exclusively in Arizona, New Mexico, and Southern California, adobe can be used effectively almost anywhere in the country, though delivery charges outside the West can make it an expensive choice. Adobe blocks commonly used in construction are made of soil, straw, water, and asphalt emulsion or portland cement. Some are formed in molds and then air-dried; others are formed in a hydraulic compressor.

With its massive form and earthy color, adobe creates a warm, informal effect in a garden living area. Because the blocks are large, building with adobe proceeds quickly,

yielding immediate results. Adobe blocks used for building are generally 16 inches long, in widths varying from $3\frac{1}{2}$ to 12 inches, and 4 inches thick. The most common block is 16 by $7\frac{1}{2}$ by 4 inches, the same as four or five clay bricks put together. Blocks can range in weight from 12 to 45 pounds.

Historically, adobe structures were doomed to decay, eventual victims of the extremes between summer heat and winter rain, although they could last longer with an occasional recoating of adobe plaster. Today's adobe blocks, however, are stabilized with portland cement or asphalt emulsion, which keeps them from dissolving. Blocks stabilized with asphalt are darker than traditional adobe blocks; those stabilized with portland cement are closer in color to the original mud and straw bricks.

Ceramic Tile

For outdoor countertops and some barbecue façades, tile is a popular choice. The range of tile available allows you to create any mood or appearance and match or complement any style. One of the oldest, most successful surfacing materials, ceramic tile is durable, easy to clean, and highly resistant to weathering.

Tile comes either glazed or unglazed. A

glaze is a hard finish, usually including a color, that is applied to the surface of the clay body (the bisque) before the final baking. Glazes can come in a high gloss, a satin-like matte, a semi-matte, and a dull, pebbly texture. Unglazed tiles do not have a baked-on finish. Their colors—commonly earth tones, ranging from yellow to dark red—are either the natural clay color or the result of pigments added prior to forming and baking.

A key consideration for tile used on a barbecue is its resistance to stains and moisture. Where stains are most likely—such as on a food preparation countertop next to a grill—opt for a glazed tile. Non-vitreous, soft-bodied tiles such as unglazed Mexican terra cotta readily absorb stains and water. You can treat them with a sealant, but this only provides a small degree of resistance.

Tiles come in many different shapes and sizes, from sheets of mosaic tiles to large pavers. To get an overview of the possibilities, spend some time in a tile dealer's showroom or home improvement center.

Though many specialty tiles are sold by the piece, most tile is priced by the square foot. When shopping, take along a clear plan that specifies the square footage you'll need so you can narrow your choices to fit your budget. This plan will also tell you the number of trim or specialty pieces required. Always buy more than what your calculations indicate—the rule of thumb is to add 5 percent for mistakes and breakage. Before you bring the tiles home, check the cartons to be sure the color in the tiles matches. Different cartons of the same tile can vary.

Tile is usually set in a bed of mortar or thin-set adhesive. See page 127 for more about installation.

Mortar

Mortar is a mixture of cement, fine sand, and water with a small amount of lime or fireclay added for plasticity. It binds masonry units such as bricks or stones together and to the base; it also binds tile to a base. Beyond this, it has several other functions: It seals out wind and water, compensates for variations in the size of masonry units, anchors metal ties and reinforcements, and provides various decorative effects, depending on how the joints are tooled.

For more about mortar, including how to estimate quantities and how to mix and use it, see page 112.

Grout

Grout, similar to mortar, is used to fill cavities in masonry barbecues, such as the cells of concrete blocks, the spaces between the wythes (rows) of bricks, and the spaces between ceramic tiles. When grout sets up, it locks surface elements together to form an essentially monolithic structure.

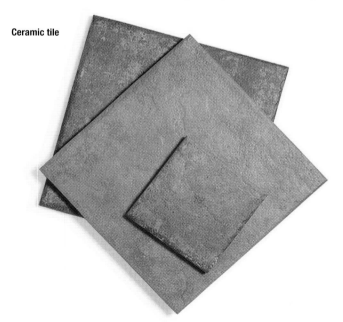

Ceramic tile

Ceramic-tile grout is sold premixed in bags—you just add water. For the amount of grout needed for a brick or concrete-block barbecue, you can mix up a thin batch of concrete (see page 108), adding pea gravel, if you wish, to fill out the mixture inexpensively; add water so the grout is just liquid enough to pour.

Cast Concrete

Cast concrete is the material of choice for barbecue footings, foundations, and slabs, and is occasionally used as a supporting slab—or even a finish surface—for countertops. Cast concrete is also a very strong, workable, flexible material for walls that have curves and other irregular shapes.

Where appearance is key—such as on a countertop—concrete can be lightly smoothed or heavily brushed, surfaced with handsome pebbles, swirled, scored, tinted, painted, patterned, or cast into molds to resemble other materials. However, producing an appearance-grade concrete finish is best left to professionals. In addition to the specialized skills required, appearance-grade concrete must be mixed to exact specifications. Once the ingredients are combined and the water added, work must proceed quickly and accurately; mistakes require extensive and, perhaps, costly removal followed by replacement. If the concrete isn't cured correctly or if surface drainage is inadequate, the surface may buckle and crack. For more about casting concrete, see page 107.

Other Structural Materials

Though barbecues tend to be built primarily from masonry materials, a variety of other

Semi-smooth

Smooth

Broomed

Rock salt

Travertine

Seeded aggregate

materials is often employed in their construction. These include wood for structural members, framing, forming concrete, and cabinetry; plywood for interior carcasses and supports for countertops; and metal for a variety of uses.

LUMBER: Woods from different trees have varying properties. Redwood, cedar, and cypress heartwoods (the darker part of the wood, cut from the tree's core) are naturally resistant to decay. This, combined with their beauty, makes them a favorite for outdoor building.

Another decay-resistant material is pressure-treated lumber—wood that has been factory-treated with preservatives that repel rot, insects, and other sources of decay. For any wood that comes in contact with the ground, use foundation-grade pressure-treated lumber. The American Wood Preservers Bureau, which governs this industry, grade-stamps pressure-treated lumber; look for the stamp before buying your lumber.

For small orders, lumber is sold by the linear foot. This designation considers only

Redwood lumber

the length of a piece. For example, four 2 by 4s, 8 feet long, are the same as 32 linear feet of 2 by 4. Be sure to list the exact dimensions of the lumber you need so your order can be filled correctly. Lumber is normally stocked in even lengths of 6 to 20 feet.

Remember that a finished 2 by 4 is not actually 2 inches by 4 inches. The nominal size of lumber is designated before the piece is dried and surfaced; the finished size is less. See the chart below for actual sizes of the nominal dimensions given to lumber.

PLYWOOD: In barbecue construction, exterior plywood is occasionally used to strengthen a structure, clad the interior of cabinetry, or build concrete forms. Standard plywood panels measure 4 by 8 feet; thickness ranges from $^1/_4$ to $^3/_4$ inch.

One problem with plywood is that the edges can delaminate when exposed to water. If, for example, you build a plywood base for a tile countertop, moisture may rise up from underneath the plywood. When it gets into the ends of the plywood, it causes swelling. As soon as this happens, the tile will pop off. Be sure to specify exterior panels or—better yet—marine-grade panels. Always treat the edges and, ideally, the surfaces with a high-grade water repellent, such as an elastomeric sealer or paint.

The appearance of a panel's face and back determines its grade. Letters A through D designate the different grades, with A being the highest.

METALWORK: A custom metal fabrication shop is a prime source for obtaining both decorative and structural parts for your barbecue. For example, as a non-combustible base for tile and mortar, one of the best materials you can use is stainless steel. Materials such as sheet stainless steel are often in stock, requiring no custom work.

A metal fabricator can also work with you to create metal doors, shelves, hardware, and other components. Though prices for raw materials such as sheet steel can be quite reasonable, custom castings and metalwork are expensive. Look up *Sheet Metal Work*, *Steel Fabricators*, or *Foundries* in your telephone book.

Masonry yards sell steel reinforcing bar and angle iron for adding strength to a masonry structure.

STANDARD DIMENSIONS OF SOFTWOODS	
Nominal size	Surfaced (actual) size
1x2	$^3/_4$" x 1$^1/_2$"
1x3	$^3/_4$" x 2$^1/_2$"
1x4	$^3/_4$" x 3$^1/_2$"
1x6	$^3/_4$" x 5$^1/_2$"
1x8	$^3/_4$" x 7$^1/_4$"
1x10	$^3/_4$" x 9$^1/_4$"
1x12	$^3/_4$" x 11$^1/_4$"
2x3	1$^1/_2$" x 2$^1/_2$"
2x4	1$^1/_2$" x 3$^1/_2$"
2x6	1$^1/_2$" x 5$^1/_2$"
2x8	1$^1/_2$" x 7$^1/_4$"
2x10	1$^1/_2$" x 9$^1/_4$"
2x12	1$^1/_2$" x 11$^1/_4$"
4x4	3$^1/_2$" x 3$^1/_2$"
4x6	3$^1/_2$" x 5$^1/_2$"

CASTING CONCRETE

A key masonry material, cast concrete is almost always used for barbecue footings and slabs, and occasionally for other structural parts and for countertops. Here we look at how to cast concrete for footings, slabs, and similar uses.

When working with concrete, proper safety equipment is a must. Everyone on the job should wear safety glasses, long sleeves and pants, and water-resistant work gloves. Spills on skin and clothing should be rinsed off immediately.

Buying Concrete

For a small project, such as the footing for a barbecue, you can make up your own concrete mix from scratch, buy a dry prepackaged mix, or haul your own plastic (wet) mix. Another option, generally reserved for large jobs, is to have ready-mix delivered by truck.

BULK DRY MATERIALS: You can save money by ordering your materials in bulk and doing your own mixing. Should you have the materials delivered? For small projects, surcharges for small-quantity delivery can eat up your savings, so if you have a truck, it's best to haul the materials yourself.

DRY PREPACKAGED MIX: Bagged, dry concrete mix is hard to beat for convenience—you just add water. Though it is an expensive way to buy concrete, prepackaged mix is certainly a labor-saver and can be economical for small jobs.

HAUL-IT-YOURSELF PLASTIC MIX: Some dealers supply trailers containing already-mixed concrete. These carry about 1 cubic yard of concrete—roughly, enough to cast 19 linear feet of a 12-by-12-inch footing plus a 4-inch-thick, 3-by-8-foot slab. The trailer may have a revolving drum to mix the concrete as you go, or it may have a simple metal or fiberglass box into which the plastic concrete is placed. A word of caution: These trailers are very heavy; be sure your tires and brakes are in good shape and that your vehicle and trailer hitch are rated for the weight.

READY-MIX: A commercial ready-mix truck is the best choice for large-scale work. The truck can deliver a large quantity, so you can finish big projects in a single placement. Locate concrete plants in the telephone book; many have minimum orders, so be sure to ask. If your construction site is far from the reach of the truck, you'll have to shuttle loads with a wheelbarrow or have the concrete pumped by a concrete-pumping contractor. The concrete pump forces ready-mixed concrete through a large hose that can be run over fences and around structures. Because of the added expense, it's only practical for large jobs or when your barbecue is part of a larger project.

Concrete-Placing Strategies

If possible, pour or "place" concrete in one fell swoop. If you must place it in stages, complete separate sections in single placements. A single placement may require several batches of concrete, but no batch should be allowed to dry before the next one is placed. Never interrupt a placement once it has begun, and remember that hot, dry weather will substantially shorten your available working time.

Because plastic (wet) concrete is essentially a liquid, it must be contained in a hole, a trench, or by concrete forms until it sets up. You can pump concrete into forms, fill forms from a wheelbarrow, either dumping (you might need a ramp) or shoveling, or dump the concrete directly from the drum of a power mixer.

This is strenuous work. Unless your job is very small, you may need some help. If you're doing your own mixing, you'll find it helpful to have others wheeling and placing the concrete.

A Concrete Formula

For most projects, this concrete formula will produce good results. Choose between the basic mix and one containing an air-entraining agent, depending on your needs.

BASIC CONCRETE: Use this formula for regular concrete. All proportions are by volume.

1 part portland cement
$2\frac{1}{2}$ parts sand
$2\frac{1}{2}$ parts stone or gravel aggregate
$\frac{1}{2}$ part water

The sand should be clean concrete sand (never use beach sand); the gravel should range from quite small to about $\frac{3}{4}$ inch in size. The water should be drinkable—neither excessively alkaline nor acidic, nor containing organic matter.

AIR-ENTRAINED CONCRETE: Adding an air-entraining agent to the concrete mix creates tiny air bubbles in the finished concrete. These help it to expand and contract without cracking, a necessity in regions with freezing temperatures. The agent also makes concrete more workable, meaning you can add less water to a batch, which makes the finished concrete stronger. An air-entraining agent should always be added to ready-mix. Specify this when you place your order.

The amount of agent you'll need to add will vary by brand, so consult your supplier, and reduce the sand to $2\frac{1}{4}$ parts.

Figuring Amounts

To calculate how much concrete to buy, refer to the table on this page. The figures include 10 percent extra for waste; you can always use any left over for steppingstones or other small projects. Note that the final volume is less than the sum of the ingredients because the smaller particles fit in among the larger ones. If you order bulk materials sold by the cubic yard, remember that each cubic yard contains 27 cubic feet.

Mixing Techniques

If your project is small, mixing the concrete by hand is the simplest method. However, for large forms that must be filled in a single placement, opt for a power mixer, keeping in mind that any mixer smaller than 3 cubic feet is more nuisance than it's worth. If you're using air-entrained concrete, you will have to use a power mixer, since hand-mixing is simply not vigorous enough to create the air bubbles needed. Whichever method you use, add the water in small increments; too much can ruin the mix.

INGREDIENTS FOR 10 CUBIC FEET OF CONCRETE	
Bulk dry material	Portland cement: 2.6 sacks Sand: 5.8 cubic feet Gravel: 6.5 cubic feet
Dry prepackaged mix	20 60-pound bags
Ready-mix	.41 cubic yards

MIXING CONCRETE BY HAND: A high-sided contractor's wheelbarrow with pneumatic tires is suitable for mixing if you don't need to work more than 1 to 2 cubic feet at a time. Or, you can simply use a large piece of plywood. Work in small batches; this will make mixing easier and give you greater control over proportions.

Ingredients for small quantities of concrete are usually measured with a shovel, which is accurate enough if your scoops are consistent. Use a container of known volume to measure the volume of a shovelful. If you need greater accuracy, you can use a bottomless (for easy dumping) 1-cubic-foot wooden box set in the wheelbarrow or on the sheet of plywood. Or, empty half a sack of cement—$1/2$ cubic foot—into a large bucket, then level and mark the bucket.

Mark another bucket off in quarts and gallons to keep track of the water. Set up so that you can bail water from a drum or garbage can, which is more convenient than turning a hose on and off.

To mix concrete, place the sand on the mixing surface and add the cement. Mix thoroughly, then add the gravel and mix again. Next, mound up the mixture and hollow out the center. Pour in the prescribed amount of water. Working around the hollow, pull the dry ingredients into the water and enlarge the size of the basin. Continue mixing until all the dry ingredients are damp.

Work a sample of the batch with a mason's trowel. The concrete should slide—not run—freely off the trowel. You should be able to smooth the surface fairly easily, and all of the large and small aggregate at the edges should be completely and evenly coated with cement.

USING A CONCRETE MIXER: Set the concrete mixer close to your sand and gravel piles so that you can shovel-feed directly; be sure the mixer is level, and chock (wedge) it in place to keep it from "walking." Read the safety information before use. If you have rented the mixer, ask for a demonstration.

To mix ingredients, add half the water and all the coarse aggregate with the mixer off. Turn it on (let it warm up on idle if it's a gas model) to scour the drum. Follow with all of the sand, along with all but 10 percent of the water. Next, add the portland cement. When the mixture is a uniform color and texture, add the rest of the water and the air-entraining agent if you're using it. After adding the final ingredients, mix for at least two minutes; continue mixing longer if necessary until the concrete achieves a uniform appearance. Always throw the ingredients from outside the rotating drum. And always thoroughly clean out and rinse the mixer immediately upon finishing work—otherwise, residual concrete will harden inside it.

CONCRETE MIXER SAFETY

Follow all safety measures recommended by the concrete mixer's manufacturer or the rental firm. Never reach into a rotating mixer with your hands or tools. Wear a dust mask and goggles, and keep well away from the moving parts.

To avoid shock hazard, an electric mixer must be plugged into a ground-fault circuit-interrupter (GFCI) outlet with a three-prong grounding-type plug and outdoor-rated three-wire extension cord. Do not run an electric mixer in wet or damp conditions.

CASTING A CONCRETE SLAB

Because of their heavy weight, most barbecues must be built on a sturdy, sound foundation. Footing size and depth may be governed by local codes—normally, the footing should be twice the barbecue wall's width (16 to 18 inches is common) and centered beneath the walls. If you live in a cold climate, sink the footings so that the bottom is at least 6 inches below the frost line.

The slab may be cast at the same time as the footings or after the footings have set up. A 4-inch-thick slab is generally ample; in areas where frost or drainage may be a problem, the slab should be poured over a 4-to-6-inch gravel bed. The slab's overall dimensions are determined by the barbecue's size. If you're building a concrete

block structure that will be veneered with stone, brick, or stucco, the slab should extend beyond the concrete block far enough to provide a support base for the veneer material.

Before casting the footings or slab, be sure to place any plumbing and electrical conduit (see pages 132–137). It's also smart to do a dry layout of your masonry units so you can precisely figure the placement of any steel reinforcing bar needed.

After casting the slab, allow it to cure properly so that the surface doesn't dry too quickly, which can cause cracking. Spray it with a light mist of water and cover it with plastic sheeting. Allow it to cure for three days—longer in cold weather.

CASTING A SLAB

The typical foundation for barbecues is actually a combination perimeter footing and slab, cast from concrete and strengthened with steel reinforcing bar and/or heavy wire mesh.

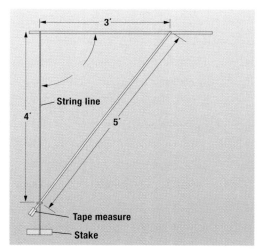

1 LAY THE FOUNDATION
A rectangular barbecue should have a foundation with corners that are at precise 90-degree angles. To be sure the corners are square, lay out a triangle with sides 3 feet, 4 feet, and 5 feet long (or any multiple of these numbers). Mark the ground with chalk or stretch strings between stakes to define the foundation's perimeter.

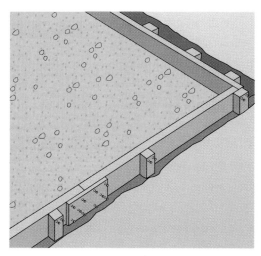

2 BUILD THE FORMS
Although trenches can serve as forms for footings, it's best to build simple temporary wood forms to contain the slab. Nail scrap 2-by-4 or 2-by-6 lumber securely to stakes. Take a little extra time when placing these to make sure their top edges are level—this will expedite finishing the concrete later.

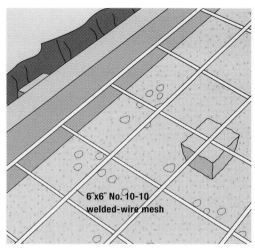

3 REINFORCE THE SLAB

To strengthen the slab, lay 6-inch-square No. 10-10 welded-wire mesh or crisscross $1/2$-inch reinforcing bar on 12-inch centers. Support the mesh or rebar about 2 inches above the base, using small pieces of brick or block.

6"x6" No. 10-10 welded-wire mesh

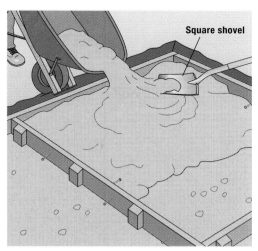

Square shovel

4 PLACE THE CONCRETE

Thoroughly dampen the soil or gravel. Beginning at one corner, place and spread the concrete. Work the mix up against the form and compact it into all corners with a shovel or mortar hoe by pushing (not dragging) the concrete. Don't overwork the material—doing so will cause the heavy aggregate to sink to the bottom.

Strikeoff

5 STRIKE THE CONCRETE

Move a straight 2 by 4 across the top of the forms to level the concrete, using a zigzag, sawing motion. Fill any voids with more concrete.

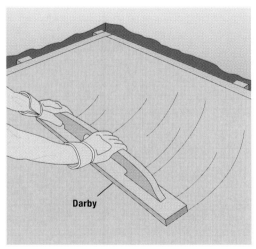

Darby

Wood float

6 SMOOTH THE SURFACE

Move a darby (which you may want to rent) in overlapping arcs, then repeat with overlapping straight, side-to-side strokes. Keep the tool flat, but don't let it dig in. After the water sheen has disappeared from the concrete but before the surface has become really stiff, smooth it again with a wood float or magnesium hand float.

MIXING & APPLYING MORTAR

Mortar, a mixture of cement, fine sand, fireclay or lime, and water, is the "glue" that binds masonry units such as brick, concrete block, and stone together. It also seals out water, compensates for the variations in irregular units, and anchors reinforcements.

Both lime and fireclay help make mortar spread easily. Fireclay has the added property of being heat-resistant, so it is used instead of lime in the mortar of a classic barbecue's firebox. Fireclay is also a better choice when building with stone because lime can stain. Many brick masons use fireclay-cement mortar throughout an entire barbecue to save the bother of preparing two types of mortar.

Recommended Formula

For either fireclay-cement or lime-cement mortar, the ratio of sand to cement is the same: 1 part cement to $4^{1}/_{2}$ parts clean, fine sand (3 to 4 parts sand for stonework). For fireclay-cement mortar, add $^{1}/_{2}$ part fireclay. For lime-cement mortar, add $^{1}/_{2}$ part hydrated lime.

ESTIMATING THE QUANTITY OF MORTAR

No. Bricks	Cement	Sand (cubic feet)	Fireclay or Lime
250	1 sack	$4^{1}/_{2}$	1 sack
500	2 sacks	9	1 sack
1,000	4 sacks	18	2 sacks

A simpler method of making lime-cement mortar is to use Type II masonry cement, which already contains lime. For fireclay-cement mortar, you can buy premixed dry mortar made with fireclay.

To make the formula from scratch, measure out the ingredients by the bag, bucket, or shovelful. Since mortar must be mixed in fairly small batches (large batches tend to harden before they're used up), masons often mix by the shovelful. The key is to be consistent in measuring so that your mortar will be the same from batch to batch.

Estimating the Quantity

For mix-your-own mortar, use the guidelines shown in the chart on this page.

A sack of cement (100 lbs.), a sack of hydrated lime or fireclay (50 lbs.), and a sack of sand (100 lbs.) equals approximately 1 cubic foot. When using dry-mix mortar, figure 50 bricks to a sack.

Mortar sand should be clean, sharp-edged, and free of impurities such as salt, clay, dust, and organic matter. Never use beach sand—its grains are too rounded and impure. Particle size should range evenly from about $^{1}/_{8}$ inch to fine. Use drinkable water, neither too alkaline nor acidic.

The amount of water added to the dry ingredients cannot be specified—it depends entirely upon the composition of the mortar, the weight and absorption rate of the masonry units, and weather conditions.

Ready for use, your mortar should have a smooth, uniform, buttery consistency. It should spread well and stick to vertical surfaces yet not smear. Mix in water a little at a time until these properties are achieved.

For concrete blocks and stones, which are heavier than bricks, make the mortar a bit stiffer so it doesn't squeeze out with the weight. Also keep in mind that the quantity of mortar needed for stonework increases sharply the rounder the stones because it must fill larger voids.

Mixing Mortar by Hand

The mortar for most masonry barbecues can be readily mixed by hand. You'll need a wheelbarrow or mortar box, and a hoe. Mix the sand, cement, and fireclay or lime thoroughly before adding water. Hoe the dry ingredients into a pile, make a hollow and add water; mix, then repeat as often as necessary to achieve the proper consistency.

Power Mixing

For a large job, use a power mixer. With the mixer running, add some water, half the sand, and all of the fireclay or lime. *Never put the shovel inside the mixer.* Next, add all of the cement, the rest of the sand, and enough water to achieve the right consistency. Run the mixer for three or four minutes after all the water is added. Mix only enough to last you about two hours.

Applying Mortar

A master mason at work is a study in skill, speed, and concentration. Try to observe one because it will give you a feel for proper technique. To lay masonry units, you need to throw a line with a trowel, as shown at right. If throwing a line is too difficult, you can cut off narrower slices of mortar and lay them down one trowel at a time.

Buttering—a self-descriptive term—is used to apply mortar to the ends of masonry units. Load a small amount of mortar onto the end of the trowel and spread it on the brick. The key to buttering is proper mortar consistency—it should be stiff enough not to drip, yet wet enough to stick.

Keep your mortar workable, or "well tempered," by sprinkling a little water as necessary and remixing. However, don't expect mortar more than a couple of hours old to revive sufficiently for use.

Allowing mortar to cure ensures that the cement and water combine chemically as the mortar hardens. To cure mortar joints, keep them moist for four days by spraying them periodically with a fine mist.

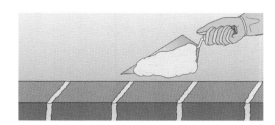

1 LOAD THE TROWEL
Place one or two shovelfuls of mortar on a wet mortarboard. Slice off a wedge and scoop it up (an 8- or 10-inch trowel holds the right amount for brickwork). Give the trowel a quick shake to dislodge excess mortar.

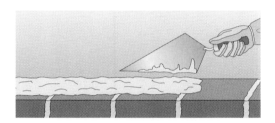

2 APPLY A LINE OF MORTAR
Bring your arm back toward your body and rotate the trowel, depositing the mortar in an even line about 1 inch thick, one brick wide, and three stretchers long, or, if you're laying headers, three headers wide. Practice on the mortarboard first until you get the knack.

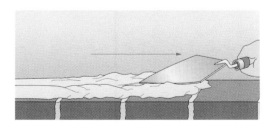

3 FURROW THE MORTAR
Once the line is thrown, furrow it with the point of the trowel. Divide the mortar, taking care not to scrape it toward you. The furrow ensures that the bricks are bedded evenly and that excess mortar is squeezed out on either side when the bricks are laid.

THROWING A LINE OF MORTAR
The technique shown here is standard for laying-up bricks and other masonry units.

BUILDING WITH BRICK

Brick is extremely popular for barbecues, no doubt because it has traditionally been used to build hearths and is one of the easiest-to-handle masonry materials. Bricks are modular in size and small enough for easy one-handed lifting. Once you get the hang of it, bricklaying takes on a certain rhythm.

This section guides you through the bricklaying techniques needed for building a freestanding brick barbecue. The instructions are for a barbecue with running bond walls (see page 101). Most barbecue walls are not built from a single width (wythe) of bricks, but from two interlocking wythes (see page 116).

Before beginning construction, you'll need to establish a concrete footing (see page 110). Your local building codes may dictate footing requirements; if not, follow these rules-of-thumb: In extreme winter climates, the footing should extend 12 inches below the frost line. In frost-free areas, a 12-inch-deep footing is sufficient for a 3-foot-tall barbecue. Bring concrete to within an inch or so of ground level. The footing should be twice as wide as the wall, and in most cases, should be centered along it. Allow the footing to cure for at least two days before building on it.

CUTTING A BRICK

Place a brick on sand or earth and tap a brickset with a hand-drilling hammer around the width of the brick. Then give the brickset a sharp blow on the scored line. Always wear safety glasses when cutting masonry.

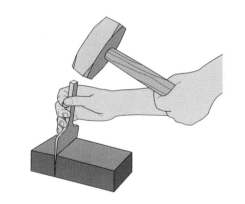

Cutting Brick

If you want really precise brickwork, or are using extra-hard bricks such as "clinkers," you'll need to rent a masonry saw or purchase a special blade for your circular saw. Softer bricks are easy to cut without a saw as shown at left.

Reinforcing Brick

A simple way to add steel reinforcement to a long barbecue wall built in running bond is to pour grout—thin, soupy concrete (see page 128)—between the two wythes. Once it has stiffened slightly, insert steel reinforcing rods into the grout right down to the footing. Or, place bars in the footing when it is poured, build around them, then grout.

REINFORCING BRICK WALLS

For large projects, reinforce brick masonry by setting Z-bar or metal ties in the mortar, as pictured at right; for long walls, pour concrete between the wythes and insert steel reinforcing rods, as shown below right.

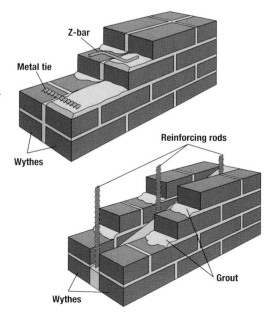

Z-bar

Metal tie

Wythes

Reinforcing rods

Grout

Wythes

Special steel ties in various patterns are made for reinforcing brick masonry—though they are not needed for small brick barbecues. Two of the most common are Z-bar and metal ties. Exact specifications and techniques for steel reinforcing are detailed in building codes; for further information consult your building department.

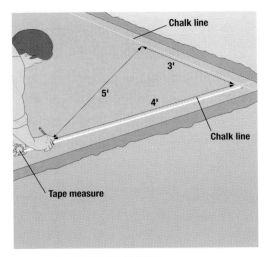

BUILDING A BRICK CORNER

Each bond pattern requires a particular corner treatment. If you choose a pattern other than running bond, you'll need to adapt these instructions.

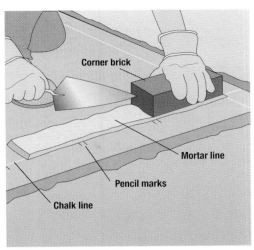

1 LAY OUT THE CORNERS
First snap chalk lines. Then check that they are absolutely square by using the 3-4-5 rule: Measure 3 feet along one line and 4 feet along the other. Now measure the distance between these two points. It should be 5 feet; if it isn't, adjust your lines.

2 START THE CORNER LEAD
After making a dry run for the entire wall (see page 116, step 2), lay the first brick exactly at the corner, lining it up carefully with your chalk lines.

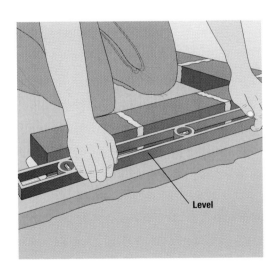

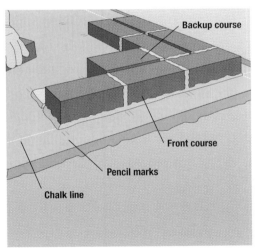

3 TAIL OUT THE LEAD
Lay the remaining four lead bricks, checking carefully for accuracy. Masons call this "tailing out" the lead. Check level and plumb, as well as the bricks' alignment, as shown. You can also use a carpenter's square.

4 LAY THE BACKUP COURSE
Throw mortar lines and lay the backup course as shown. Make sure not to disturb the front course, and remember that there is no mortar joint between these courses. Be sure that the backup course is level with the first one.

(continued on page 116)

BUILDING A BRICK CORNER

(continued from page 115)

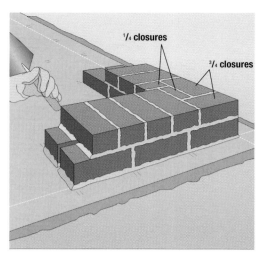

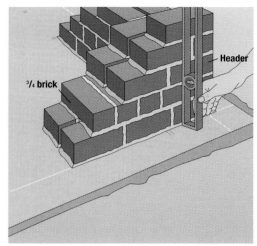

5 START THE HEADER COURSE
Take two bricks and cut them into $3/4$ and $1/4$ pieces. These are known in the building trade as "closures." Lay them as shown and complete the lead header course.

6 COMPLETE THE LEAD
Now lay the leads for the next three stretcher courses. Note that each of these courses is the same as the first course, except the fourth course, which begins with a header. Check your completed lead for accuracy, and repeat these steps for the other corners of the barbecue. Now you're ready to finish the barbecue between leads, as shown on the facing pages.

BUILDING BRICK BARBECUE WALLS

After pouring the footing as discussed on page 110, distribute your bricks along the site in stacks. Hose them down several hours before you begin to prevent them from absorbing too much moisture from the mortar. Save any broken bricks for cut pieces. Place a hose or bucket nearby for rinsing your tools as you work and for keeping your mortar well-tempered (see page 113). Make constant checks with a level and measuring tape as you go. Sight down the wall periodically to make sure it's true.

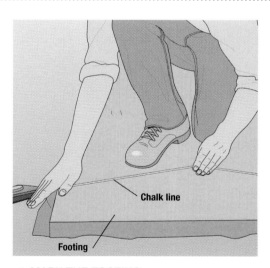

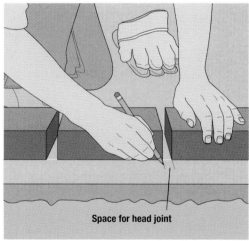

1 MARK THE FOOTING
To make sure the walls are centered, locate the outer edge of each wall by measuring in from the edge of the footing, first at one end, then the other. For each wall, stretch a chalk line between the two points and snap it to mark your guidelines.

2 LAY A DRY COURSE
Lay a single course of bricks along each chalk line the full length of each wall, allowing $1/2$-inch spaces for the head joints. If possible, adjust the head joint width to allow you to lay the course without cutting any but the header bricks. Mark the brick spacing on the footing with a pencil.

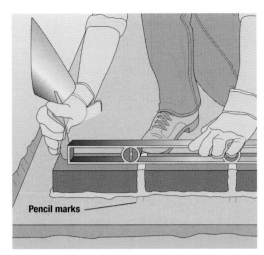

Pencil marks

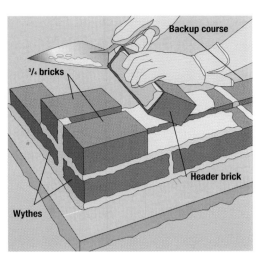

Backup course

³/₄ bricks

Header brick

Wythes

3 LAY THE FIRST BRICKS

Take up the bricks from the dry course. Throw a mortar line (see page 113) three bricks long and lay the first three bricks. Butter the head-joint ends of the second and third bricks and place them with a shoving motion so that the mortar is squeezed out of all sides of the joint. Use a tape measure to check the course for correct height, check plumb and level, then tap the bricks into place. Trim off any excess mortar.

4 BEGIN BACKUP COURSES

Lay three backup bricks just as you did the first three. Use your level to check that the courses in each wythe are the same height, and use a brick to check the overall width of the wall. Butter just enough of the inside edge of the first backup brick to seal the end of the two wythes, as shown. Cut two ³/₄ bricks to begin the header course, again buttering a bit of the inside edge of the backup brick, then lay three header bricks.

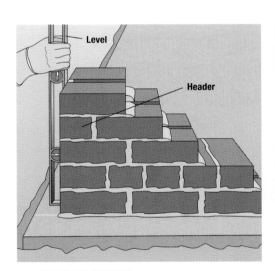

Level

Header

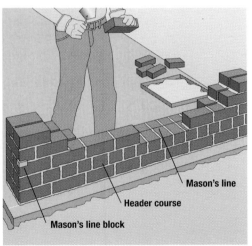

Mason's line

Header course

Mason's line block

5 FINISH THE LEAD

Continue laying stretchers until the lead is five courses high, as shown. (Note that the fourth course begins with a single header.) Use your level to check that the lead is true on each of its surfaces. Now go to the other end of the footing and build another lead.

6 FILL IN

Stretch a mason's line between the completed leads, then, begin laying the outer course. Keep the line about $1/16$ inch away from the bricks and flush with their top edges. Lay bricks from both ends toward the middle. Once you reach the top of the leads, shift the mason's line to the back of the wall and begin laying the backup courses.

FINISHING MORTAR JOINTS

If your job is small, tooling, or "striking," mortar joints can be left until the end. For larger jobs, though, you'll need to do this periodically as you work. Mortar joints should be struck with a striking tool when they are thumbprint hard.

Try to keep mortar and dirt away from unit faces as you work. If brushing proves insufficient, wash with a solution of trisodium phosphate (TSP) or a non-phosphate substitute and laundry detergent. (Try ½ cup of each to 1 gallon of water.) Rinse well.

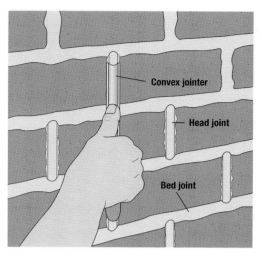

1 STRIKE THE JOINTS
First, press or draw a striking tool vertically along each head joint as shown. Then run the striking tool horizontally along the bed joints.

2 CUT OFF TAGS AND BRUSH BARBECUE
Slide your trowel along the barbecue to remove the mortar that has been forced out of the joints, called tags. When you've finished, restrike the bed joints. Once the mortar is well set, brush the barbecue with a stiff broom or brush; this will eliminate the need for cleaning later on.

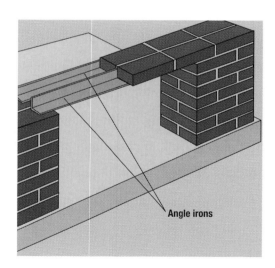

Angle irons

SUPPORTING BRICK ABOVE AN OPENING

When building a barbecue from brick, you're likely to encounter a situation where the brick must span an opening—usually above a cabinet or storage area. At each side of the opening, build the wall up to the opening's top edge. Bridge the opening with a length of 3- to 4-inch steel angle iron, supporting it at each end as shown. Mortar this in place where it will be hidden by the bricks that run across the opening. Allow the mortar to set up, then continue building the wall.

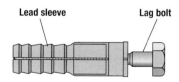

Lead sleeve   Lag bolt

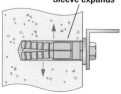

Sleeve expands

FASTENING TO CONCRETE

You can use concrete nails for lightweight attachment to concrete and concrete block, but a more secure method is to use an expanding concrete anchor. Using a drill or hand-drilling hammer and a masonry bit, drill a hole the diameter of the sleeve and slightly longer. Then tap the sleeve in. Slip a lag screw through the fixture to be attached, and tighten it into the sleeve.

APPLYING STUCCO

Stucco is a durable masonry finish favored for many barbecues, particularly by people with stucco-sided homes. Stucco is a mixture of cement, sand, lime, and water churned into a thick paste and troweled onto a base in three coats: a scratch coat, a brown coat, and a finish coat. The finish coat may be textured or smooth and is usually colored or tinted.

With house construction, stucco is typically applied over sheathing paper containing metal lath or mesh that has been attached to the wall studs. But because wood is combustible, most stucco-clad barbecues are built using some other method. Homeowner-built types, in particular, are generally constructed from concrete block or brick that is then coated with the stucco.

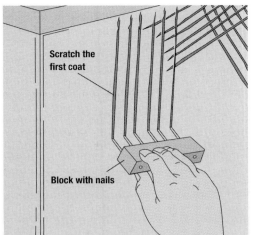

1 APPLY THE FIRST COAT
Spray the surface of the concrete block with water. Using a mason's trowel, apply the first, or "scratch," coat approximately $1/2$ inch thick. Press it firmly to the base with the trowel in sweeping arcs. When it is firm, scratch the surface as shown to provide "tooth" for the next coat. Allow the first coat to cure for two days, occasionally misting it with a fine spray of water.

PREPARING TO STUCCO

For the scratch and brown coats, buy bagged stucco mix. Add $1/10$ part lime for easier workability and mix with enough water to make a fairly stiff paste. For the final coat purchase a stucco color coat mix in the desired shade. Plan to do the work when the weather is mild—neither freezing nor sweltering.

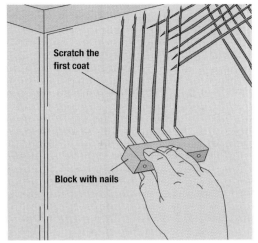

2 APPLY THE BROWN COAT
Apply the second, or "brown," coat, about $1/4$ inch thick over the dampened first coat. Draw a metal straightedge across the surface to flatten it. Then use a metal float to even it out (work it until water surfaces). Let the coat cure for two days, keeping it moist with a fine mist.

3 FINISH WITH THE COLOR COAT
Apply the finish, or "color," coat over the dampened brown coat with a metal float. For a smooth texture, just draw the float across the surface. For other textures, daub a sponge or brush on the surface, or splatter with more stucco and smooth down high spots. (If you plan to texture it, do this within half an hour of application.) Spray a fine mist on the surface and cover it with plastic sheeting. Allow it to cure for about four days.

BUILDING WITH CONCRETE BLOCK

Concrete blocks, also called "concrete masonry units," or "CMUs," are an excellent material for barbecue building. They are non-combustible, relatively large, and designed to be easily assembled with mortar. For more about concrete block, see page 100.

Concrete blocks may be left exposed, but they more often provide the structure for barbecues that are faced with slate, tile, brick, stone, or other materials. Here we look at how to build a basic wall from concrete block. You may want to review the information about building with brick, beginning on page 114, because many of the techniques are similar.

CONSTRUCTION BASICS: Use the same mortar used for brick (see page 112), but keep it a little on the stiff side so it won't squeeze out of the joints. Do not wet the blocks prior to laying them, as you do bricks. The stiffer mortar and the blocks' relatively low rate of absorption will keep them from absorbing too much water from the mortar. Also, wetting makes blocks expand; when they dry they may shrink, causing the barbecue to develop cracks.

CUTTING CONCRETE BLOCK: When cutting any kind of masonry, always wear safety glasses or, better still, a face shield. The best tool for cutting concrete block is a hand grinder with a carbide wheel—you just dip in to cut it. This is particularly useful for cutting-in electrical boxes. If you don't own a hand grinder, you can rent one.

HOW TO BUILD WITH CONCRETE BLOCK

Concrete blocks, like brick, are installed on a footing, as discussed on page 110. Allow the footing to cure for at least two days, then mark the foundation the same way as for laying brickwork (see step 1 on page 116). Corners should be interlocked. See step 1 on page 115 for corner layout techniques.

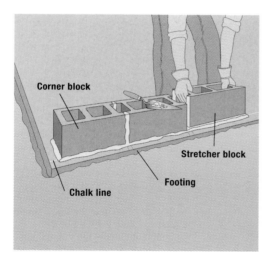

Corner block

Stretcher block

Footing

Chalk line

1 START THE LEAD
Lay a 2-inch-thick mortar bed long enough for three or four blocks. Lay the corner block carefully and press it down to create a 3/8-inch joint with the foundation. Butter the ends of the next blocks and place them to allow for a 3/8-inch joint. Check the lead for alignment, level, and plumb.

2 COMPLETE THE LEAD
Continue as for bricklaying (see page 117), beginning even-numbered courses with perpendicular blocks and mortaring the face shells. For maximum strength, mortar both the face shells and webs, making full bed joints. When one lead is finished, go to the other end of the wall and build the second lead.

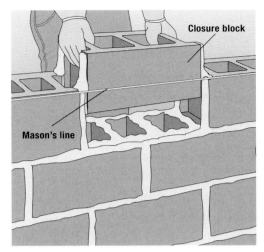

3 FILL IN BETWEEN LEADS
Lay blocks between the leads, keeping an accurate ³/₈-inch joint spacing. Check alignment, level, and plumb frequently. To fit the closure block, spread mortar on all surfaces of the opening and on the ends of the block, then carefully set it in place.

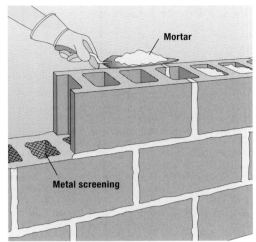

4 CAP THE BARBECUE
You can make a simple cap by filling the cores of the top course with mortar. First, cover the cores of the next-to-last course with ¹/₄-inch metal screening or building paper, making sure it doesn't interfere with the bond between the face shells. Then, lay the top course and finish by adding the mortar to the cores.

You can also cut concrete block using a circular saw with a masonry cutoff blade. Make a series of cuts, increasing the depth with each successive pass. Place the saw's base plate on the block, taking care to keep the power cord clear of the saw's path. Turn the motor on and, once the saw has reached full speed, carefully follow the scored line. Do not force the blade, and stop if the saw vibrates or makes any unusual noise. Once through the cut, turn the saw off, wait for the blade to stop, and unplug the saw. Adjust the blade for the next cut.

If you don't have any power tools, you can just score a block with a brickset and break away the unwanted piece with a few hammer blows just as you would a brick (see page 114).

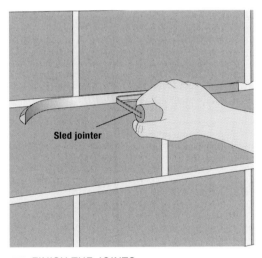

5 FINISH THE JOINTS
For maximum strength, make a compacted concave or V-shaped joint between the blocks. A long sled jointer like the one shown is best, but a smaller jointer, or even a dowel, will do. Tool the vertical, then the horizontal joints, working from bottom to top. Finish by knocking off tags (excess mortar) with your trowel (see page 118).

BUILDING WITH STONE

More than any other masonry material, stone lends a feeling of natural permanence to a structure. Stonework ranges in appearance from the casual look of countryside rubble walls to the formality of exactly fitted ashlar masonry. For more about stone, see page 101.

Because stone is irregular in shape, walls made of stone tend to be less stable than those built of brick or concrete block. For stability, stone walls are generally built thicker than are brick or concrete block walls. Or stone is applied as a veneer to another material such as concrete block (see page 120 for information on building with concrete block).

CONSTRUCTION BASICS: Because stone barbecues cannot be reinforced easily, building codes in regions subject to earthquakes generally discourage stone masonry if the structure will be taller than 3 feet. Construction may be restricted to facing a reinforced concrete-block barbecue with a façade of stone.

Plan to establish a concrete footing (see page 110) that will extend below the frost line, or, if you live in a frost-free area, 12 inches deep. Bring concrete to within an inch or so of ground level. The footing should be about half again as wide as the wall. Allow it to cure for at least two days.

A solid stone wall is typically built of a double thickness of stones with rubble fill—small stones and chips—in between, as shown in step 1 on the facing page. The walls should slope toward the center—this inward tilt is called "batter," and it helps secure the wall since the faces lean on each other. A good rule of thumb is 1 to 2 inches of batter for every 2 feet of rise, less if the stones are very regular. Ashlar stonework does not require batter.

If you decide to face a concrete-block structure with stone, adapt these instructions to apply a single layer of stone.

CUTTING STONE: To fit an awkwardly shaped stone, you can trim simply by hammering at the stone with a bricklayer's hammer. If you need to cut a stone, use a stone chisel or brickset. Score a line completely around the stone, working with its natural fissures, and tap the chisel with a hand-drilling hammer. Then drive the chisel against the line to break the stone apart. Always wear safety glasses when cutting stone.

MORTAR: The mortar formula for stonework contains more cement than that for brick and concrete block (see page 112): 1 part cement to 3 or 4 parts sand. Add $1/2$ part fireclay for workability, but don't add lime (or use mortar cement, which contains lime) because it can stain the stones. Keep the mortar somewhat stiffer than for brick or block. The quantity of mortar needed will increase sharply the rounder the stones.

Because of its large joints and voids, a stone wall may consist of as much as one-third mortar. Laying a sample section will be your best guide to mortar requirements.

Because of their weight, very large stones can squeeze out most of the mortar in their bed joints. To preserve the joint spacing, support them on wooden wedges. After the mortar has stiffened, you can pull out the wedges and pack the holes with mortar. Stone chips may also be used as wedges, and they do not need to be removed.

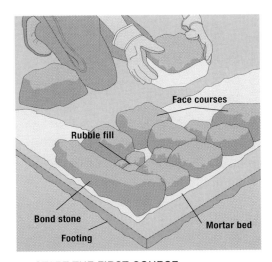

Face courses

Rubble fill

Bond stone

Footing

Mortar bed

1 START THE FIRST COURSE

Lay a 1-inch-thick mortar bed for the first bond stone and set it in place. Work only with clean, dry stones (dirt and moisture will interfere with the bond). Continue, mortaring the edges of the stones before laying them. Pack the head joints (vertical joints) with mortar after setting the stones.

2 LAY ADDITIONAL COURSES

For each subsequent course, build up a mortar bed and set the stones in place just as you did with the first course. Work slowly, dry-fitting stones before throwing down the mortar. You can save mortar by filling large joints with small stones and chips. Check the wall's alignment and plumb or batter as you go.

HOW TO BUILD WITH STONE

For a massive, natural-looking barbecue, build with stone. But be aware that it is very difficult to install built-in grills, storage cabinets, appliances, and the like into this type of structure. As a more flexible alternative, face a concrete block structure with a single layer of stone. Corners should be interlocked the same way as corners built of brick or block (see page 115).

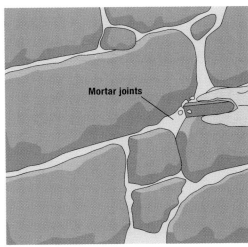

Mortar joints

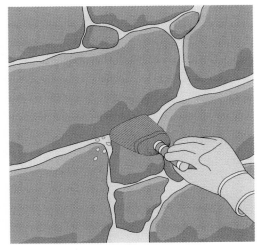

3 RAKE THE JOINTS

After you've laid a section, rake out the joints to a depth of $1/2$ inch to $3/4$ inch with a piece of wood. Deeply raked mortar joints enhance the play of light and shadow on the face of the wall. Ashlar stone barbecues can be struck as for brick (see page 118).

4 CLEAN UP

As you work, wipe spilled mortar from the face of the stone with a wet sponge. After the mortar joints are tooled, use a whisk broom to remove crumbs of mortar. Once the mortar has dried, wash the barbecue with clear water. If this doesn't remove all the residue, try soapy water and a clear rinse. Don't use a steel brush because it could mar the stone.

BUILDING A COUNTERTOP

An outdoor countertop provides a convenient surface for preparing food and contributes significantly to the beauty and style of a barbecue. As discussed on page 103, an array of countertop materials is available—though most recommended for outdoor use are tile or thin, flat masonry materials such as cut stone. An outdoor countertop must be durable, stain resistant, and able to withstand the elements. In addition, it should shed water and be non-combustible. The most common constructions are shown on page 126.

Most grill manufacturers specify that combustible materials be distanced several inches from the grill, firebox, and any other heat source. Local codes may also restrict the use of wooden supports. Be sure to refer to codes and manufacturer instructions before constructing any part of your barbecue. In fact, buy your barbecue grill, sink, and other appliances before building the barbecue and countertop.

Providing Support

A barbecue or outdoor kitchen's countertop spans the top of the structure, so the bed must be a flat, slablike surface strong enough to carry the load. When planning your barbecue's height, normally about 36 inches, be sure to figure in the countertop's entire thickness, including tile or other masonry units, the mortar bed (if this is the method you're using), and the supporting base.

SUPPORT FRAME: Unless you're installing a solid stone or concrete-slab countertop, you will need to build a support frame (see below). A couple of ways to do this are:

For a wood frame, install cedar, redwood, or pressure-treated 2 by 4 or 2 by 6 supports between the barbecue's walls, anchoring them to ledgers bolted to the walls with masonry anchors. For the typical 24-inch-deep countertop, space the front-to-back rails no more than 24 inches apart. Be aware that the gas grill industry recommends a 24-inch clearance between a barbecue grill and any combustible materials, which rules out wood framing in many situations.

To build a non-combustible frame, you can use steel. The easiest option is to use steel wall studs, as discussed in the project on page 38. You can use a power circular

SUPPORT FRAMES

Sturdy framing carries the weight of a barbecue's counter. Shown here are a wood frame (right) and non-combustible steel frame (far right).

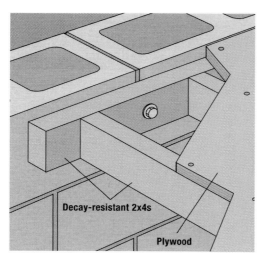

Decay-resistant 2x4s

Plywood

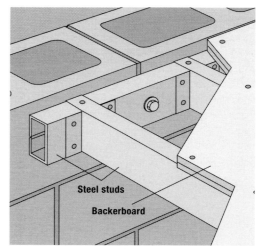

Steel studs

Backerboard

saw equipped with a composition metal-cutting blade to cut them and self-drilling steel-framing screws to join them (be sure to wear safety glasses when cutting and drilling metal). Another option is to build the frame from steel angle iron, welding or bolting the pieces together. If you must drill holes in steel, drill slowly, lubricating the metal-drilling bit with oil as you go.

PLYWOOD: Indoor countertops usually have plywood as the base for mortar or thin-set adhesive and tile or other countertop surface materials. Exterior or marine-grade plywood can be used outdoors in regions where the climate is predominantly dry. When exposed to moisture, plywood can swell or delaminate—especially along edges—so be sure to treat it with an elastomeric paint or sealer. Keep in mind that plywood is a combustible material, so it is governed by the same rules as frame materials discussed above.

To make a plywood base, lay $3/4$-inch exterior-grade plywood across the top support frame, attaching it with 2-inch galvanized deck screws spaced 6 inches apart around the edges and 8 inches apart along the mid-panel rails. Where plywood pieces butt up to each other, leave about $1/8$-inch space to allow for expansion. Also leave a $1/8$-inch gap between the plywood and the barbecue's back wall. If you intend to top the plywood with a mortar bed and tile (or a similar material), be sure to cover it with a layer of building paper, overlapping the edges about 6 inches.

CEMENT BACKERBOARD: This fire-resistant panel product, a concrete fiberglass-rein-forced backing made specifically for use with tile and similar materials, is essentially a thin piece of concrete sandwiched between pieces of fiberglass mesh. It creates a solid bond with both thin-set adhesive and mortar, though this bond can be undermined if the backerboard becomes saturated with water. Cement backerboard usually is sold in $1/4$-, $7/16$-, or $1/2$-inch-thick panels measuring 3 by 4 to 3 by 6 feet. Where strength is an important consideration, you can stack two panels together.

Backerboard can be scored and snapped or cut with a power saw equipped with a blade designed for cutting concrete and stone. Fasten it to the plywood and/or supporting frame with $1 1/2$-inch galvanized screws spaced 6 inches apart along the edges. To keep moisture out, cover it with a waterproof membrane, sold as a kit consisting of reinforcing fabric and liquid rubber, and follow the manufacturer's instructions to apply it. Some masons recommend applying a cement backerboard over the top of plywood; this is a technique used indoors, but freezing temperatures outdoors may cause tiles to pop off.

STAINLESS STEEL: One of the most durable—but costly—materials you can use as a base for tile or other masonry countertops is sheet stainless steel. It can be ordered to size from sheet metal dealers. Choose a thickness that will span the supports without deflecting under the weight of the countertop material—typically about 12 gauge. You can apply mortar right on the stainless steel or, like some masons, apply "blue glue," a thin concrete bonding agent that improves adhesion, before the mortar.

CONCRETE SLAB: A 3- or 4-inch-thick steel-reinforced concrete slab makes a sturdy, flat, non-combustible base. It is cast the same way you would cast a slab on the ground (see page 110), except that you create it on top of the barbecue walls. Cut a few pieces of ³/₄-inch plywood to make a base that will fit inside the barbecue walls. Support this base with a temporary ledger of short 1 by 4s or 2 by 4s around the inner perimeter of the walls, fastened with concrete nails as shown on page 124.

Install #3 or #4 reinforcing bar, crisscrossed on 12-inch centers and supported by small pieces of brick, 1¹/₂ inches above the plywood. Remove the ledger and plywood pieces after the concrete sets up (pull out the pieces through doorway or appliance openings in the lower part of the barbecue). See the project on page 74 for a variation of this method that can be used to create a slab top on a curved barbecue.

Another option is to install precast concrete steppingstones, sold in 3-by-3-foot sizes at many home improvement centers. Use a masonry blade in a power circular saw to cut them to size (be sure to wear safety glasses). Make progressively deeper cuts until you can break away the excess with a brickset and a hand-drilling hammer. To fasten the pieces in place, drill 2-inch-deep holes in the top of the wall, then insert short bolts or metal studs and epoxy them into the holes. Place the steppingstone pieces on top of the studs to mark matching holes on their undersides. Drill these shallow holes to receive the bolts or studs.

STONE SLAB: At a stoneyard, you may be able to find slabs that are large enough to serve as single-piece countertop sections.

TYPICAL COUNTER BASES

Tile and other countertop materials require a sturdy, durable base. Three popular choices are heavy-gauge stainless steel (top), steel-reinforced cast concrete (right), and precast concrete steppingstones (far right).

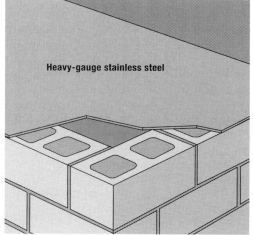

Heavy-gauge stainless steel

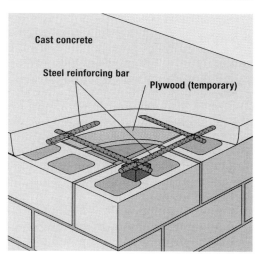

Cast concrete

Steel reinforcing bar

Plywood (temporary)

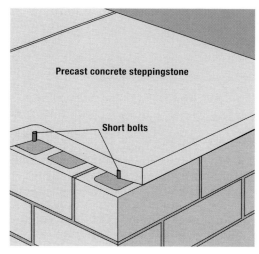

Precast concrete steppingstone

Short bolts

Cut them (or have them precut to size by the stone dealer) and fasten them to the barbecue walls with exterior-grade epoxy as discussed above for concrete steppingstones.

Tiling a Surface

The instructions that follow refer specifically to ceramic tile; however, stone tile is installed similarly. Heavy, thick, or irregular materials should be installed on a mortar base. Whether you use the thin-set adhesive method or a mortar bed, installing tile and similar masonry units requires providing a base or backing as discussed on page 125, spacing and laying the tile or units, then grouting and sealing.

PLANNING THE LAYOUT: If you plan to install a sink in the counter, mark its center point with a pencil and draw a straight line from front to back on the plywood. If you are not installing a sink, draw straight lines from front to back at the counter areas' midpoints (assuming counter on both sides of the grill). Place a dry run of edge and field tiles, starting with full tiles along the front edge and working back. Allow the appropriate space for cove tiles if the counter includes a backsplash. If no backsplash is planned, leave a $1/8$-inch gap between the last counter tile and the back wall or back edge.

Use plastic tile spacers for accuracy. Work from the marked centerlines outward so that any cut tiles will be of equal measurement on the ends. If less than half a tile is indicated at the ends, move the centerline the equivalent of one-half tile in either direction. Do not tile over the edge of the sink or grill holes because the weight of the fixture will flip it up. Once you're happy with the tile placement, mark the location of key tiles on the base, then pick them up and stack them nearby.

SETTING EDGE TILES: Set the edge trim first. If you are using cove tiles for a backsplash, set them in place after the edge-trim units, making sure to line them up so the grout lines will run straight. (See the illustrations on page 128 for instructions on marking and cutting tile. See page 122 for information on cutting stone.)

SETTING SINK TRIM: A self-rimming sink goes in after you have set all of the tile, but a recessed sink is installed before the field tiles are set. Once you have placed the sink and caulked carefully between the sink and the backing, you are ready to set the trim tile around it.

SETTING FIELD TILES: After you have set all the trim pieces, lay the field tiles. If you have installed a sink, work from it outward; otherwise work from the center of the counter outward. Use spacers if the tiles do not have integral spacing lugs. Check the grout joint alignment frequently with a straightedge to maintain straight lines. To bed and level the tiles, place a small piece of plywood over several tiles at a time and tap gently with a mallet or hammer.

TILING THE BACKSPLASH: If you used cove tiles at the bottom of the backsplash, set the field tiles on the wall, working from the center outward. If you did not use cove tiles, set the field tiles on the wall, one grout width above the counter tiles. Use bullnose tiles if the backsplash is only one row or for the top row of tiles. For this row, apply adhesive to each tile before setting it in place. If the wall contains electrical outlets, cut the tile to fit around their boxes, removing the cover plates after turning off the power to the circuit. Before resetting the cover plates, bring the outlets out flush with the tile.

MARKING TILE

You can mark the backside of tile with a pencil, or the surface with a felt-tip pen. Transfer angles with an adjustable T-bevel, as shown, or use a combination square to mark a 90-degree cut.

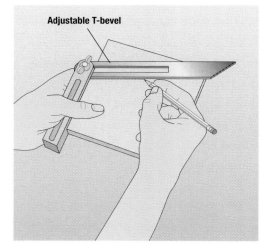

Adjustable T-bevel

CUTTING TILE

For a small barbecue project, a snap tile cutter (at right), which most tile dealers rent or lend, can speed making straight cuts. Just position the tile, pull the handle toward you while pressing down firmly to score the surface, then press down on the handle to break the tile. When cutting tile, always wear safety glasses. To cut small bits of tile, use tile nippers, as shown below right.

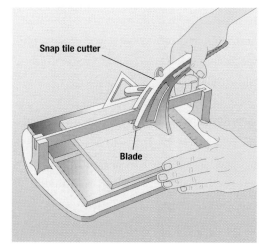

Snap tile cutter

Blade

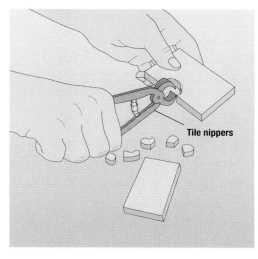

Tile nippers

PREPARING FOR GROUT: As the tile sets, clean any excess adhesive from the tile faces and barbecue surfaces. Once the adhesive has dried thoroughly, or cured as indicated by the instructions (24 hours is generally the minimum), you are ready to grout the tiles.

APPLYING THE GROUT: Scrape any remaining adhesive out from between the tile joints. Mix the grout according to the manufacturer's instructions. Properly mixed grout should be the consistency of cookie dough. Grout should sit just below the tile surface to show the tile in relief, but not so low it will be difficult to wipe away crumbs.

CLEANING UP: Cleaning grout off tile can be tricky. You want to remove excess grout before it dries yet not disturb the grout lines as they firm up. Once the grout has dried, polish the tile with a soft, clean cloth.

SEALING: Unglazed tile is absorbent so it needs to be sealed to protect it from staining and from the elements. Before applying a sealer, wait at least two weeks to allow the grout to cure completely. Both tiles and grout should be clean and completely dry before sealing. Follow the manufacturer's instructions for applying the sealer, which usually involves spreading it on, then wiping off any excess or film. Since the sealer often leaves an unwanted shine on the tile, be sure to wipe each tile clean immediately after applying the sealer.

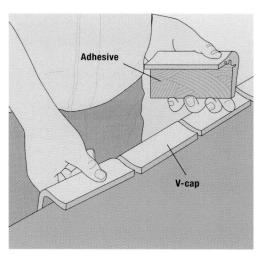

Adhesive

V-cap

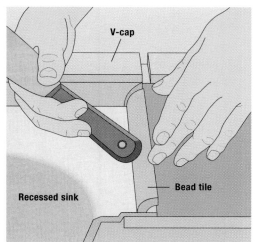

V-cap

Recessed sink

Bead tile

HOW TO TILE A COUNTER

This sequence shows the method for applying ceramic tile to a base with thin-set adhesive. Other countertop materials may be applied using similar methods.

1 SET EDGE TILES

Apply a thin layer of adhesive to both the back of the tile and the counter edge by raking it on with a notched trowel in a squiggle pattern. Press the first tile into place with a slight twisting motion and press firmly. If the edge trim consists of two pieces instead of the one-piece V-cap, set the vertical piece on the front of the counter first. Secure with masking tape until the adhesive sets.

2 SET SINK TRIM

On a recessed sink, use the centerline on the backing as the starting point and work from front to back. Liberally spread adhesive on one trim piece at a time. Tap each carefully into place with the back of the spreader. If you are setting a bead trim, set the pieces at the sink corners first.

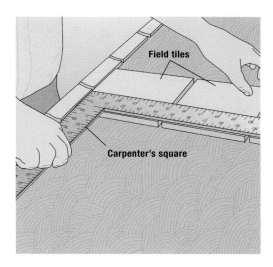

Field tiles

Carpenter's square

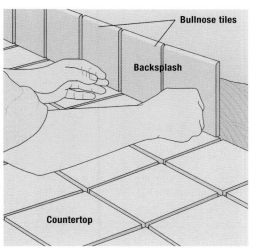

Bullnose tiles

Backsplash

Countertop

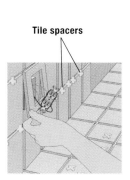

Tile spacers

3 SET FIELD TILES

Using a notched trowel, spread adhesive over a 2-foot-square section of counter. Lay the field tiles from front to back, placing them with a slight twisting motion. Use spacers if the tiles do not have integral spacing lugs, and check the grout-joint alignment frequently with a straightedge. To bed and level the tiles, place a small piece of plywood over several tiles at a time and tap gently with a mallet or hammer.

4 TILE THE BACKSPLASH

Spread adhesive on the wall to just shy of the desired tiling height and apply adhesive to each tile before setting in place. If the wall contains electrical outlets, cut the tiles to fit around their boxes (inset). Be sure to turn off the power to the circuit first, remove the cover plates, and bring the outlets out flush with the tile.

(continued on page 130)

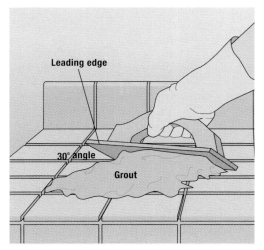

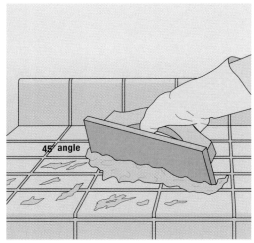

5 **APPLY THE GROUT**
With a rubber-backed trowel, spread about a cup of grout across a section of tiles no more than 5 feet square. Holding the leading edge of the trowel at about a 30-degree angle, spread the grout firmly over the tile. Work the trowel back and forth at different angles to force the grout into the joints so that no voids or air pockets exist.

6 **REMOVE THE EXCESS**
After grouting a tile section, scrape off the trowel and go over the section again to pick up any excess. Hold the trowel at a 45-degree angle to the surface and draw it diagonally across the joints. Clean the trowel frequently in a bucket of water as you work.

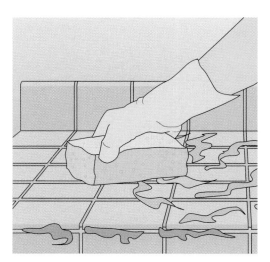

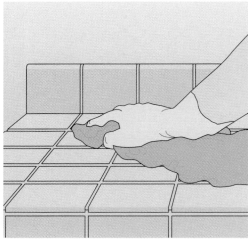

7 **CLEAN GROUT FROM TILES**
Wipe across the tile at an angle to the grout lines with a damp sponge, rinsing it frequently in clear water. If the grout seems too soft, move on to another area, then come back. When the tiles appear as clean as possible, let the grout dry.

8 **POLISH THE SURFACE**
When the grout has hardened and a haze has appeared on the tile surface, wipe off each tile with a soft clean cloth, taking care not to disturb the grout joints. If grout has ridden up onto some tiles, use the back of an old toothbrush or a small stick wrapped in a cloth to clean along the tile edges. When the entire surface is clean, let the grout dry overnight.

One of the great features about contemporary prefabricated gas grills is that they're easy to install. With most it's just a matter of sliding or dropping the unit into a countertop recess and hooking up the gas line.

Your best reference for installing a grill properly and safely is the owner's manual for your grill. Pay special attention to all warnings and cautions. Working with natural-gas piping can be dangerous—a leak can release gas vapors that are toxic, highly flammable, and, when contained in an enclosed space, explosive. If you have any doubts about your ability to hook up gas plumbing properly and safely, defer to the services of a plumber or your gas utility provider.

The instructions given here assume that a plumber roughed-in a gas line to the barbecue's location and installed a gas shut-off valve before the foundation was poured. The gas pipe—normally $\frac{1}{2}$ inch in diameter—should be stubbed up beneath the grill where both assembly and valve are easily accessible. Be sure to follow the grill's specifications and consult with local codes for proper pipe size and location of the gas line.

Caution: Be sure the gas is turned off at the meter before making any connections or working on the gas piping.

If a gas pipe can't be routed to the barbecue's location easily, plan to install an LP/propane-fueled grill, which will require space for proper tank storage in a well-vented area (normally beneath the grill).

Be sure to allow for all minimum clearances from combustible materials such as wood when installing the grill.

The methods and fittings for connecting a grill to the gas shutoff valve will depend upon the grill's makeup. A typical connection is shown below. Note that a gas regulator connects to the barbecue; be sure the arrow indicating the direction of gas flow points toward the unit.

Wrap the male threads of threaded fittings with approved pipe-wrap tape or pipe-joint compound (don't use on flare fittings).

When all connections are secure, turn the gas back on—but leave the burners off—and check for leaks. Brush or spray a mixture of soapy water onto all connections, supply hoses, and pipes. Escaping gas will create bubbles. If bubbles appear, turn the gas off and tighten the fittings, then retest. Never use a flame to check for gas leaks.

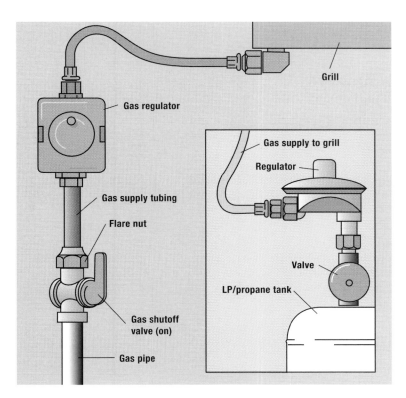

TYPICAL GAS CONNECTION
Gas-supply tubing connects to the shutoff valve and regulator in this typical connection that utilizes copper tubing with flare fittings. Other types use a gas hose with threaded fittings. An LP/propane-tank hookup requires a regulator/hose assembly, as shown (inset).

PLUMBING AN OUTDOOR KITCHEN

A sink adds a world of functionality to a barbecue area—in fact, it is usually the component that advances the simple barbecue to "outdoor kitchen" status. On these pages, we'll look at how to put a sink and its plumbing into a barbecue unit.

Working with water piping is relatively easy, assuming a water-supply pipe and drainpipe have been roughed-in at the site (you may want to consult with or have a plumber do the rough-in work). Be sure to have the necessary pipes roughed-in before the barbecue unit's slab or foundation is cast. Here are the requirements:

WATER SUPPLY: For cold water, it is usually easiest to tap into a water pipe where it serves a nearby outdoor hose bibb or faucet. For hot water, a supply pipe must run from the barbecue's sink to an existing hot water pipe or the hot water heater. Or, you can install a small, on-demand hot water heater.

An electric "on-demand" instant hot water heater—a very small plug-in unit that is installed under a sink—can be an excellent alternative to running a hot water pipe from the home's hot water heater to your barbecue's sink. The unit connects to a cold water pipe and heats the water as it travels through the unit to the faucet. A thermostat on the unit controls the water temperature. Units vary by the size of the heating elements' wattage, from 500 to 1,300 watts. They're sold with installation directions and specifications.

ROUGHING-IN PLUMBING

The typical setup of utilities beneath a barbecue's counter involves several components. The sink has two $1/2$-inch copper pipes with shutoff valves located about 22 inches off the ground. An additional gate valve allows you to shut off the water before an on-demand water heater to simplify repairs. A $1 1/2$-inch ABS plastic drainpipe with a P-trap (or S-trap) is centered directly beneath the sink. In addition, this illustration shows the electrical conduit and the gas supply.

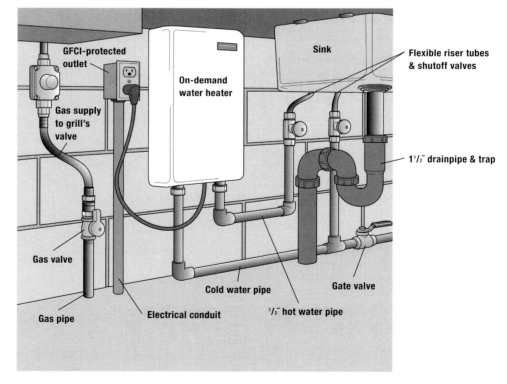

GFCI-protected outlet

Sink

Flexible riser tubes & shutoff valves

On-demand water heater

Gas supply to grill's valve

$1 1/2$" drainpipe & trap

Gas valve

Cold water pipe

Gate valve

Gas pipe

Electrical conduit

$1/2$" hot water pipe

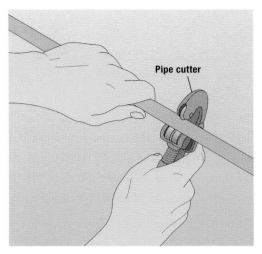

1 CUT THE PIPE
Use a pipe cutter to make cuts, twisting the knob until the cutter wheel makes contact with the surface. Rotate the cutter around the tube, tightening after each revolution, until the tube snaps in two. After you've cut the pipe, clean off inside burrs with a round file, and file or sand off outside burrs. Use #00 steel wool to polish the last inch of the pipe and the inside of the fitting down to the shoulder.

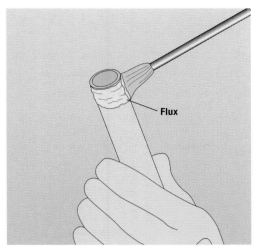

2 APPLY SOLDERING FLUX
With a small, stiff brush, apply sweat-soldering flux around the polished inside of the fitting and outside pipe end. Avoid getting any flux on your hands as it can be caustic. Place the fitting on the end of the pipe. Turn the pipe or the fitting back and forth to spread the flux evenly.

MAKING A SOLDERED JOINT

Plumbing with copper pipe involves sweat-soldering lengths of pipe together with copper fittings. To sweat-solder a joint, you'll need a small propane torch, some #00 steel wool, very fine sandpaper or emery cloth, a can of soldering flux, and lead-free plumber's solder.

DRAIN: Route drainage from the sink to a nearby existing drainpipe that ties into the sewer or septic system. If this isn't possible, you may be able to simply drain the sink into a small pit filled with drain rock. Check local codes about restrictions.

Working with Copper Pipe

Even when a plumber has roughed-in the water supply, it's often necessary to run some copper pipe to serve the sink and—if you have one—the on-demand water heater. On this page is a brief look at basic techniques for working with copper pipe.

Cut new lengths of copper pipe with a pipe cutter designed for the job. You can also cut copper pipe with a fine-toothed hacksaw or mini-hacksaw (24 to 32 teeth per inch), but it's more difficult to make a straight, clean cut with a saw than with a pipe cutter. To determine the amount of

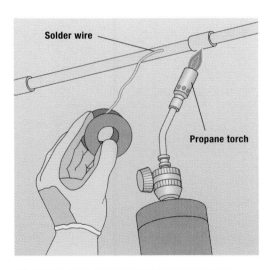

3 HEAT THE FITTING & APPLY SOLDER
Position the fitting and move a torch flame back and forth across it to distribute heat evenly. Touch the solder wire to the joint as you're heating—when the wire melts, the joint is ready. Remove the torch and touch the solder to the fitting's edge so capillary action pulls molten solder into the joint. When solder shows all the way around the fitting, stop. After the joint cools, carefully wipe off surplus flux with a damp rag—the pipe will still be very hot.

copper pipe you need, measure the distance between the fittings, then add the distance the pipe will extend into the fittings. Always wear safety glasses and work gloves while cutting and soldering copper pipe.

STRAINER ASSEMBLY

A sink strainer has several parts assembled both above and below the sink.

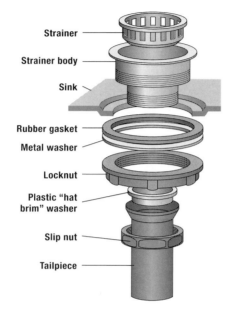

Strainer
Strainer body
Sink
Rubber gasket
Metal washer
Locknut
Plastic "hat brim" washer
Slip nut
Tailpiece

Installing a Sink

When installing a sink in a new countertop, you'll need to provide a hole, or "cutout." If the countertop has a concrete or stone slab beneath its surface material, the cutout will need to be made during construction. A stone mason can cut the stone or you can cast a concrete slab with a hole formed for the sink.

Sinks are sold with a template or pattern for the cutout. Locate the cutout according to the manufacturer's directions—normally, about $1^{3}/_{4}$ inches from the countertop's front edge. Avoid placing the sink directly over a cabinet side or other obstacles.

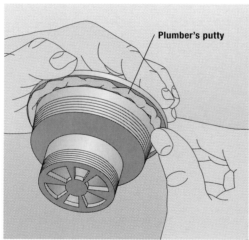

Plumber's putty

1 PREPARE THE SINK'S DRAIN
Install the drain assembly in the sink's drain hole first. To do this, place a bead of plumber's putty around the bottom edge of the strainer's lip, then press the body into the drain hole (some types have a rubber washer instead that seals the strainer).

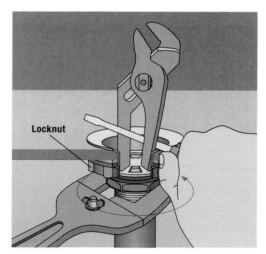

Locknut

2 TIGHTEN THE STRAINER
From the sink's underside, push the rubber gasket and metal washer onto the strainer body and hand-tighten the large locknut. Place the handles of a pair of pliers in the strainer and hold a screwdriver between the handles for counterforce while you tighten the nut. Wipe any excess putty from the sink's surface.

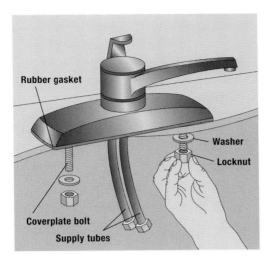

Rubber gasket

Washer

Locknut

Coverplate bolt

Supply tubes

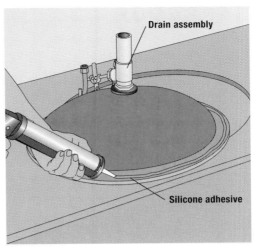

Drain assembly

Silicone adhesive

3 INSTALL THE FAUCET
Following the faucet manufacturer's instructions, feed the supply tubes through the sink and fasten the faucet in place. Most faucets have a gasket that goes on the bottom; if yours does not, apply plumber's putty around the edges before setting the faucet in place. Turn the locknuts onto the faucet inlet shanks or coverplate bolts by hand, then tighten with a basin wrench.

4 SET THE SINK
Place the sink upside down and run a bead of silicone adhesive along the underside of the molded lip (or use the adhesive included with the sink). Turn the sink over and carefully set it in place. Make sure the sink's edge is aligned with the countertop's front edge. Press firmly around the lip to form a good seal. After the adhesive has set, seal between the sink and counter with a bead of latex caulk, then smooth it with a wet finger.

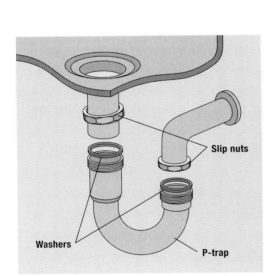

Slip nuts

Washers

P-trap

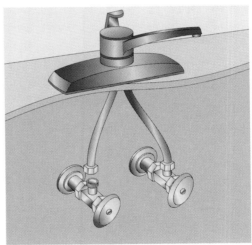

5 ATTACH A TRAP
Sink traps are sold as complete units with washers, threaded slip nuts, and the fitting itself. Choose either a P-trap or an S-trap, depending upon the roughed-in drainpipe and code requirements. Slide the new slip nuts and washers on over the sink's tailpiece to connect it to the drainpipe. Set the trap in place and tighten the slip nuts at both ends by hand. With a spud wrench (or tape-wrapped slip-joint pliers), finish tightening. Be careful not to strip or overtighten the slip nuts.

6 ADDING SHUTOFF VALVES
Shutoff valves simplify turning off the water supply to the sink for repairs. Buy brass shutoff valves sized to fit both the supply pipe and the riser tubes. Choose from either straight or angled styles, depending on the location of the supply pipes. Buy the type with female threads and screw them on to soldered male fittings (first apply pipe-wrap tape). Gently bend the supply tubes to meet the shutoff valves and join them using compression nuts or flared fittings.

WIRING A BARBECUE

Most of this book's outdoor cooking centers feature electrical outlets as part of their accouterment. Outlets are necessary for small appliances, charcoal starters, rotisseries, refrigerators, and more. Here we look at how to install and wire receptacles. For more complex wiring, use an electrician.

These instructions assume that an electrician has roughed-in an electrical circuit that runs from the house's electrical service to the barbecue's location. If you'll be installing only one or two receptacles to serve small appliances, you may be able to draw the power from an existing outdoor receptacle—just be sure the circuit can handle the increased load. The wiring should be roughed-in before the barbecue's concrete slab and footing are cast; otherwise, you'll have to run electrical conduit through one of the barbecue's walls.

Check with your local building department about any necessary permits, inspections, or restrictions. Before beginning work on any wiring, be sure to shut off the power to the circuit by removing the fuse or switching off the circuit breaker. Then, tape the circuit breaker in the OFF position, or lock the service panel.

Materials

Because outdoor wiring must withstand the elements, outdoor electrical materials are stronger and more resistant to corrosion than those used for indoor wiring. Also, because outdoor components must fit together tightly to prevent water from entering them, heavy-duty gaskets or special fittings often seal coverplates on outdoor electrical boxes.

An outdoor receptacle is in a watertight housing box. These boxes are made of cast aluminum, zinc-dipped iron, or bronze and have threaded entries to keep out water. All covers for watertight boxes are sealed with gaskets—and many switch boxes are equipped with an exterior on/off lever that enables you to operate the switch without opening the cover.

To carry the power from the house to the barbecue, underground feeder cable (type UF) is commonly used. It is waterproof and can be buried directly in the ground, although it's sometimes run through conduit for additional protection from water and physical damage. For wiring receptacles in most barbecues, a cable with two No. 12 conductors and a ground conductor running

PVC housing box

PVC conduit

Prebent 90° angle

T condulet with pull cover

PVC straps

Coupling

through a ³/₄-inch-diameter conduit is usually sufficient.

Rigid nonmetallic (PVC schedule 40)
conduit is the most popular type for outdoor
use where codes permit the use of plastic
conduit, and it is the best choice for direct
burial because it is lightweight and doesn't
corrode. PVC conduit comes in 10-foot
lengths, each with one coupling for joining it
to additional lengths. Other fittings are available for configuring runs, including
90-degree angles and condulets that allow
for a T connection.

Special PVC housing boxes are designed
for use with plastic conduit (they are different
than the plastic electrical boxes used for
indoor electrical cable). Nonmetallic conduit
does not constitute a grounded system so you
must run a separate grounding wire or cable
that includes a separate ground conductor.

Installing Conduit & Cable

Cutting lengths of PVC conduit and joining
them together with fittings is easy work.
You can cut PVC conduit with a hacksaw,
handsaw, or pipe cutter. After cutting, trim
the ends inside and out with a pocket knife
to remove any rough edges. Glue conduit
and fittings together with gray conduit
cement (not the water pipe cement used
with PVC irrigation pipe).

Fasten the conduit and boxes to the
inner walls of the barbecue within 4 feet of
each box or fitting. Straps and housing
boxes should be fastened to the masonry
with concrete nails or masonry anchors.
Push the wire or cable through the conduit
(for long runs of conduit, you may have to
rent or buy a "fish tape" to draw the wire
through the conduit).

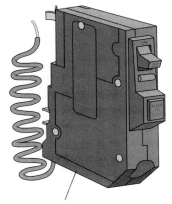

GFCI circuit breaker

GFCI receptacle

GROUND-FAULT CIRCUIT INTERRUPTERS

To prevent accidental
shock, codes specify
that any new outside
receptacle be pro-
tected with a
ground-fault circuit
interrupter (GFCI). A
GFCI circuit breaker
may be installed in the
service panel to protect
the entire circuit, or a
GFCI receptacle may
be installed right at the
barbecue. The latter
method is less expen-
sive in most cases; the
receptacle is pro-
tected, as are any
other receptacles
installed in the circuit
from that point onward
(called "downstream").

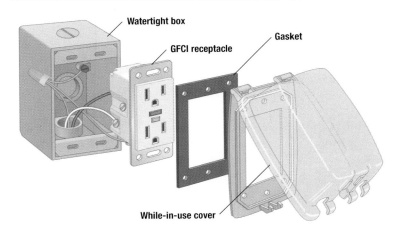

Watertight box

GFCI receptacle

Gasket

While-in-use cover

INSTALLING A RECEPTACLE

Wire the receptacle as shown above. When wiring a receptacle, use a wire nut to
connect the ground wires to the receptacle's ground and the electrical box's
green screw (if it has one). Connect the white wire to the silver terminal or white
wire on the receptacle and the black wire to the brass terminal or black wire.
Finish installation and affix the coverplates before turning the power back on.

FUELS & STARTERS

CHARCOAL BRIQUETTES: Long the outdoor chef's favorite fuel, charcoal briquettes are manufactured from pulverized charcoal and additives that make them easy to light. Once ignited, briquettes provide good, even heat, but the various brands differ somewhat in composition and density. Top-quality brands burn longer and more evenly. Store briquettes in a dry place.

SELF-STARTING BRIQUETTES: Impregnated with a liquid starter, these briquettes ignite with a match and heat up quickly. Do not add self-starting briquettes to a hot fire—the fuel in them burns off slowly and can spoil the flavor of the food. Always use regular briquettes when additional charcoal is needed.

The method you choose for starting a charcoal fire is largely a matter of personal preference—all are effective.

LIQUID STARTER: If you use a liquid starter, be sure it's a product intended for charcoal, and follow the manufacturer's instructions closely. Let the starter soak into the coals for a few minutes, then ignite in several places. Never pour liquid starter on hot coals—this can cause a dangerous flare-up.

SOLID STARTER: Solid starters are safe, non-toxic, odorless cubes or sticks that light easily with a match and burn without further attention. Mound the briquettes in a pyramid shape on top of the cubes, leaving a corner of the cubes exposed. Ignite the cubes and the coals will be ready in 25 to 30 minutes.

CHIMNEY STARTER: The metal canister on this device holds a supply of charcoal briquettes a few inches above the charcoal grate. Light some wadded newspapers underneath the chimney, and it will quickly bring the coals to readiness.

ELECTRIC STARTER: Comprised of a large heating element, a handle, and an electrical cord, this device nestles in a bed of unlit briquettes and ignites them when the cord is connected. After 10 minutes, remove the starter (if you leave it in too long, the heating element will burn out).

LIQUID PROPANE AND NATURAL GAS: Gas barbecues use either liquid propane or gas as fuel. Liquid propane is stored in a refillable tank mounted on the barbecue grill. Expect 20 to 30 hours of use from a tank. Natural gas is piped to a grill through a permanent hookup to a gas line. *Never use one kind of fuel in a barbecue grill designed for the other.*

BONELESS CHICKEN AND TURKEY

Place food on cooking grate, using Direct Method for a charcoal grill, Indirect Method/Medium Heat for a gas grill. Cook for time given in chart, based on medium-well 170°F, or until meat in thickest part is no longer pink; turn once halfway through cooking time.

Type of Poultry	Thickness or Weight	Approximate Cooking Time
Chicken		
Breasts	4–5 oz each	10 minutes
Breast cubes	1 inch	10–12 minutes
Turkey		
Tenderloins	About 6 oz each	10–12 minutes
Breast slices	¼ inch thick	3–5 minutes
Breast cubes	1 inch	12–15 minutes

BONE-IN PIECES & WHOLE BIRDS

Place food on cooking grate, using Indirect Method for a charcoal grill, Indirect Method/Medium Heat for a gas grill. Cook bone-in pieces, bone side down, for time given in chart or until no longer pink near bone; sear first, if desired. Cook whole birds, breast side up, for time given in chart or until an instant-read thermometer inserted in thickest part (not touching bone) registers 180°F; begin checking doneness 30 minutes before minimum cooking time.

Chicken		
Whole	3½ –4 lbs	1–1½ hours
Halves	1½–1¾ lbs each	50–60 minutes
Breast halves	About 8 oz each	30–35 minutes
Drumsticks, thighs	4–6 oz each	35–45 minutes
Wings	About 3 oz each	30 minutes
Rock Cornish Game Hens		
Whole	1–1½ lbs	45–60 minutes
Halves	8–12 oz each	35–45 minutes
Turkey		
Whole	10–13 lbs	1½ –2¼ hours
	14–23 lbs	2½–3½ hours
Breast halves	3–3½ lbs each	1–1½ hours
Drumsticks, thighs	1–1½ lbs each	55–65 minutes
Duck		
Whole	4–5 lbs	1½ –2 hours
Farm-raised, halves	12–16 oz each	30–35 minutes

DIRECT & INDIRECT METHODS OF COOKING

Direct Method: When using a charcoal grill, spread hot coals in a single solid layer that fills the charcoal grate. Place the food on the cooking grate directly over the hot coals. Place the lid on the grill, leaving all vents open, and grill as directed by your recipe, turning the food once halfway through the cooking time. When using a gas grill, turn all burners to HIGH, and preheat 10 to 15 minutes to bring the grill to 500°–550°F. Then adjust the controls as the recipe directs (use for pre-heating and searing).

Indirect Method: When using a charcoal grill, pile hot briquettes as close as possible to the out-side edges of the barbecue (use fuel holders if you have them). Place a foil drip pan on the charcoal grate between the coals. Arrange food in the center of the cooking grate and grill as directed with the lid on and vents open. If using a gas grill, follow the directions in your owner's manual. With most, arrange food in the center of the cooking grate, place the lid on the grill, and set the burners to MEDIUM (turn the center OFF on a three-burner grill).

BEEF

Place steaks on cooking grate, using Direct Method for a charcoal grill, Indirect Method/Medium Heat for a gas grill. Cook for the time listed in this chart, based on medium-rare (145°F), or until desired doneness; turn once halfway through the cooking time. Sear, if desired.

Cut of Meat	Thickness or Weight	Approximate Cooking Time
Steaks (T-bone, New York,	1 inch	10–12 minutes
porterhouse, tenderloin, top	1½ inches	14–16 minutes
round, sirloin, rib-eye, fillet)	2 inches	20–25 minutes
Flank steak	1–2 lbs	12–15 minutes
Skirt steak	¼–½ inch	7–9 minutes

VEAL & LAMB

Place chops on cooking grate, using Direct Method for a charcoal grill, Indirect Method/Medium Heat for a gas grill. Cook for time given in chart, based on medium (160°F) for veal and medium-rare (145°F) for lamb, or until desired doneness; turn once halfway through cooking time. Sear, if desired.

Veal chops (rib, loin)	¾ inch	10–12 minutes
	1 inch	12–14 minutes
	1½ inches	16–18 minutes
Lamb chops (rib, loin, shoulder)	1 inch	10 minutes
	1½ inches	12–14 minutes

PORK

Place chops on cooking grate. On a charcoal grill, use Direct Method for ¾-to-1-inch thickness, and the Indirect Method/Medium Heat for thicker chops. On a gas grill use Indirect Method/Medium Heat for all chops. Cook for time given in chart, based on medium (160°F), or until meat near bone is no longer pink; turn once halfway through cooking time. Sear, if desired.

Chops (rib, loin, shoulder)	¾ inch	10–12 minutes
	1 inch	12–14 minutes
	1¼–1½ inches	25–35 minutes

BURGERS & SAUSAGES

Place patties or sausages on cooking grate, using Direct Method for a charcoal grill, Indirect Method/Medium Heat for a gas grill. Cook for time given in chart, based on medium (160°F) for ground beef, lamb, and pork and medium-well (165°F) for ground chicken and turkey, or until desired doneness; turn once halfway through cooking time.

Lean ground beef, lamb, pork	¾ inch	10 minutes
Lean ground chicken, turkey	¾ inch	10–12 minutes
Sausages (uncooked), Italian,	1 inch in diameter	18–20 minutes
bratwurst, chicken, turkey, or		
other gourmet-type meat		
combinations		

SEAFOOD FILLETS, STEAKS, & BONELESS CUBES FOR KEBABS

Place fish on cooking grate (support less-firm fillets on heavy-duty foil), using Direct Method for a charcoal grill, Indirect Method/Medium Heat for a gas grill. Cook for time given in chart or until fish is opaque but still moist in thickest part; turn once halfway through cooking time (unless fish is on foil).

Type of Seafood	Thickness or Weight	Approximate Cooking Time
Fillets	½ inch	6–8 minutes
	¾ inch	8–10 minutes
Fillets and steaks	1 inch	10 minutes
Boneless cubes for kebabs	1 inch	8–10 minutes

WHOLE FILLETS & WHOLE FISH

Place whole fillets and whole fish, skin side down, on cooking grate (support less-firm fish on heavy-duty foil), using Direct Method for a charcoal grill, Indirect Method/Medium Heat for a gas grill. Cook for time given in chart or until fish is opaque but still moist in thickest part.

Whole fish fillets	1½ inches	20 minutes
Whole fish	1–1½ inches	10–15 minutes
	2–2½ inches	30–35 minutes
	3 inches	45 minutes

SHELLFISH

Place shellfish on cooking grate, using Direct Method for a charcoal grill, Indirect Method/Medium Heat for a gas grill. Cook crab, lobster, shrimp, and scallops for time given in chart or until opaque in thickest part; turn once halfway through cooking time. Scrub and rinse live clams, mussels, and oysters; cook until shells open.

Crab, whole (precook for 5 minutes)	About 2½ lbs	10–12 minutes
Lobster, whole (precook for 5 minutes)	About 2 lbs	8–10 minutes
Lobster tails	8–10 oz	8 minutes
Shrimp		
Large	Under 30 per lb	4–5 minutes
Colossal (also called prawns)	10–15 per lb	6–8 minutes
Extra-colossal (also called prawns)	Under 10 per lb	8–10 minutes
Scallops	1–2 inches in diameter	5–8 minutes
Clams, hard-shell	Medium size	5–8 minutes
Mussels	Under 12 per lb	4–5 minutes
Oysters	Small	8 minutes

FIRE SAFETY

Follow the manufacturer's instructions carefully and heed the rules below to ensure grilling safety.

- Never leave a hot grill unattended. Keep children and pets at a safe distance.
- Never use a charcoal or gas grill indoors or in a closed garage or enclosed patio.
- Do not use gasoline or other highly volatile fluids as charcoal lighters.
- Do not add liquid starter to hot—or even warm—coals.
- Place your grill in an open, level area away from the house, wood railings, trees, bushes, or other combustible surfaces.
- Do not barbecue in high winds.
- Wear an insulated, fire-retardant barbecue mitt and use long-handled tools designed for grilling.
- Do not wear clothing with loose, flowing sleeves.

RESOURCES & CREDITS

INFORMATION

Barbecue Industry Association
710 E. Ogden Ave., Ste. 600
Naperville, IL 60563-8614
(630) 369-2404
www.bbqind.org

Barbecue'n On The Internet
(888) 789-0650
www.barbecuen.com

Barbeques Galore
15041 Bake Pky., Ste. A
Irvine, CA 92618
(949) 597-2400
www.bbqgalore.com

Big Green Egg
3414 Clairmont Rd.
Atlanta, GA 30319
(800) 939-3447
www.biggreenegg.com

Broilmaster Division of
Martin Industries Inc.
301 E. Tennessee St.
Florence, AL 35630
(800) 255-0403
www.broilmaster.com

Char-Broil
P.O. Box 1240
Columbus, GA 31993
(800) 352-4111
www.charbroil.com

Ducane Co.
800 Dutch Sq. Blvd., Ste. 200
Columbia, SC 29210
(800) DUCANES
www.ducane.com

Dynasty Range
7355 E. Slauson Ave.
Commerce, CA 90040
(800) 794-5233
www.dynastyrange.com

Ironworks
P.O. Box 578
Stockbridge, MI 49285
(800) 811-9890
www.topgrill.com

Marvel Industries
P.O. Box 997
Richmond, IN 47375-0997
(800) 428-6644
www.marvelindustries.com

Mugnaini Imports, LLC
11 Hangar Way
Watsonville, CA 96706
(888) 887-7206
www.mugnaini.com

National Barbecue Association
P.O. Box 9685
Kansas City, MO 64134
(816) 767-8311
www.nbbqa.org

Prochef Inc.
2440 Railroad St.
Corona, CA 91720
(800) 771-2922
www.prochef2000.com

Robert H. Peterson Co.
14724 East Proctor Ave.
City of Industry, CA 91746
(626) 369-5085
www.rhpeterson.com

Viking Range Corp.
111 Front St.
Greenwood, MS 38930
(888) 845-4641
www.vikingrange.com

Weber-Stephen Products Co.
200 E. Daniels Rd.
Palatine, IL 60067
(847) 934-5700
www.weberbbq.com

Wolf Range Co.
19600 S. Alameda St.
Compton, CA 90221
(800) 366-9653

W W Wood, Inc.
P.O. Box 398
Pleasonton, TX 78064
(830) 569-2501
www.woodinc.com

PHOTOGRAPHS

ASN Natural Stone, 14 middle & bottom

Barbeques Galore, 15 top, 16 top right, 17

Robert Chartier, 99, 100, 102, 103

Glenn Christiansen, 18

Peter Christiansen, 25 bottom

Crandall & Crandall, 11, 12, 13, 19 top, 21 bottom left & upper right

Beth Faso, 3 middle, 29 bottom right

Fireclay Tile, 104

Ken Gutmaker, Cover, 42, 78, 86

Jamie Hadley, 1, 22 top & bottom right, 58, 59, 62, 75

David Hewitt & Anne Garrison, 3 top, 5

Art Gray, 8

Philip Harvey, 7, 20, 26, 29 top, 46, 50, 91, 106

Peter Malinowski, 19 bottom

Jack McDowell, 105

E. Andrew McKinney, 9, 22 top left, 30, 34, 54, 55, 66, 67, 74, 82, 90

Norman A. Plate, 70, 71, 72

Mark Rutherford, 136

Ann Sacks Tile & Stone, 14 top

Chris Shorten, 138, 140

Thomas J. Story, 38

David Wakely, 6

Weber-Stephen Products Co., 15 bottom, 16 bottom left, 25 top

Tom Wyatt, 3 bottom, 95

BARBECUE DESIGN

Bertotti Landscaping, Inc., 9

City Building Inc., 75

Dennis Tromburg Associates, 65